Classic Furniture Projects

Books by A. W. Marlow

THE CABINETMAKER'S TREASURY *(with F. E. Hoard)*
available in paperback as
GOOD FURNITURE YOU CAN MAKE YOURSELF
FINE FURNITURE FOR THE AMATEUR CABINETMAKER
THE EARLY AMERICAN FURNITUREMAKER'S MANUAL
CLASSIC FURNITURE PROJECTS

Classic Furniture Projects

A·W·MARLOW

Stein and Day

NEW YORK

Acknowledgments

Photographs by Bruce Mervine, Yorktowne Studio, Inc., York, Pa.

First published in 1977
Copyright © 1977 by A. W. Marlow
All rights reserved
Designed by Herb Johnson
Printed in the United States of America.
Stein and Day/*Publishers*/Scarborough House,
Briarcliff Manor, N.Y. 10510

Library of Congress Cataloging in Publication Data

Marlow, Andrew W
    Classic furniture projects.

    1. Furniture making—Amateurs' manuals.   I.   Title.
TT195.M359   684.1'04   76-54800
ISBN 0-8128-2184-X

Contents

Preface

IT IS with pleasure and a great deal of satisfaction that we present to the reader a book consisting of the necessary instructions, photographs, and line drawings that will direct him in his efforts to create really outstanding furniture.

Inlaid furniture is unbelievably less difficult to make than one may imagine. Compared to carved designs or those with many curved features, Classic Inlay, with its straight lines, offers fewer problems than any of the familiar styles.

Inlay is an aspect of furniture-making that, for no apparent reason, has been mostly overlooked by all of us who feel qualified to influence the serious amateur. The more people learn about inlaid furniture, by reading and practicing the simple techniques required, the more their interest and appreciation of this furniture style will increase.

We believe that virtually every furniture builder, with or without much experience, wants to be assured that he can add inlaying to his woodworking knowledge and do it with little extra effort or additional equipment. This assurance is given here without reservation because there are no special skills needed over and above those required for any other furniture style.

Building Classic Inlaid furniture is certainly not restricted to the advanced woodworker. In fact, up to the point of inlaying the designs, construction could not possibly be simpler since straight lines are employed. Actual inlaying requires only care in the use of hand tools and a little extra thought when you're selecting the primary wood you'll use in construction.

Mahogany offers excellent contrast to the inlay woods but requires more experience when staining and finishing than does walnut or cherry. Walnut, with few exceptions, is ideal construction wood.

Helpful Information

PRESUMABLY you are interested in making one or more of the pieces shown in this book. Before you actually start, you can avoid irritating delays by having on hand at least these two suppliers' comprehensive catalogues:

Albert Constantine & Son, Inc.
2050 Eastchester Road
Bronx, NY 10461   50¢ in stamps

Craftsman Wood Service Co.
2727 South Mary Street
Chicago, IL 60608   50¢ in stamps

Almost everything you will need can be found itemized in either one, even planed lumber although that should be far less expensive if procured locally.

Another catalogue that will be helpful when brass hardware, special locks, and hinges are needed is available from:

Ball & Ball
463 West Lincoln Highway
Exton, PA 19341 $1.00

The most used lumber thickness is 4/4, or one inch in the rough. If purchased from a lumber dealer in a reasonable board foot quantity, in random widths and lengths, surfaced two sides to 13/16", the cost will be the lowest possible per board foot. If you have a stock of wood on hand, it will be no problem to choose a piece, saw it to the required width, and re-saw (see below) it to thickness.

You should know this about glues. Hide glue is the traditional bonding agent, and many still prefer it. It's usually sold in granulated form these days for mixing in hot water. Its chief advantage is quick setting, but that can be a definite drawback when you need to coat large surfaces that require a lot of time before clamping. You can also buy hide glue in ready-mix form. It comes in a can and is used cold, just as it is. This agent sets much more slowly than the hot variety.

Casein is a dry powder you mix with cold water. It serves well when you need a slow-setting glue. Be warned though that it can stain woods like walnut and cherry. And remember that a new batch of that adhesive must be mixed every day. It doesn't keep. Many old timers like casein despite what others see as its faults.

This survey of glues isn't meant to be exhaustive. Contact cement, for example, is a relatively modern adhesive, and it doesn't need clamp pressure for bonding. You'll no doubt find one of the many new brands of ready-mix and powder adhesives convenient and satisfactory in those instances you need a bonding agent.

Readers seeking more sources of supply would do well to subscribe to *Fine Woodworking,* a quality magazine that features an annually updated as complete as possible, list of supply houses. For latest subscription rates write to The Taunton Press, P.O. Box 355, Newtown, CT 06470.

Tools

If your workshop doesn't already include the following tools, you should acquire:

A portable router with straight bits, size 1/16″, 1/8″, 3/16″, 1/4″, 3/8″, and 1/2″.

A portable 3″ belt sander to take medium and fine sand belts.

A fine-toothed back saw (sometimes called a dovetail saw) and an extra-fine-toothed saw for mitering inlay banding.

A simple, small miter box made especially for mitering inlay banding.

An inexpensive extra marking gauge with the point carefully filed to channel 1/16″ inlay grooves on concave curved surfaces where the router would be ineffective.

Here are a few definitions that may help some readers to better understand the written instructions.

Re-saw

To reduce a thicker board to two thinner pieces by holding the board "edge up" on the circular or band saw.

Glue setting

Setting the work aside to allow the glue to harden has been variously referred to as: "set overnight," "overnight setting," "lay aside for setting," "after glue setting." Overnight means from 8 to 12 hours. This applies to all kinds of glue.

Rout out

To remove wood to a uniform depth in a given area. To prepare a surface for an inlay insert.

Wood grain direction

Three dimensions often referred to—length, width, and thickness—are related to grain direction. Length is always with the grain, width across the grain. Sometimes the length may be less than the width.

Primary wood

The visible wood of which furniture is made is called primary. Any interior parts are called secondary.

Classic Furniture Projects

I

Portable Desk

MATERIALS

    2 walls 5-16″ x 2 13-16″ x 12″
    2 walls 5-16″ x 2 13-16″ x 9″
    2 panels (top and bottom) 5-32″ x 9″ x 12″
    liner wood 3-32″ x 2½″ x approximately 42″
    tray ⅜″ x 1½″ x 11½″
    plywood bed ¼″ x 8½″ x 11½″

INLAY

    string (holly) 1-28″ x 1-16″ 3-ft. lengths (2)
    ¼″ banding 3-ft. lengths (3)
    one quarter rounds 1¼″ (4)
    oval 6⅝″ x 3½″ (1)

HARDWARE

    ¾″ narrow brass butt hinges (3)
    brass box corners (4)

As I said earlier, the best woods for inlaying are mahogany, walnut and cherry. Unless you have easy access to mahogany, walnut is first choice with cherry a close second.

You needn't be an antique enthusiast to enjoy making one of these coveted desks. They are useful on occasion and are great conversation pieces.

This box was made of walnut and was chosen for chapter 1 because it illustrates miter and spline corner construction. The two box projects in the

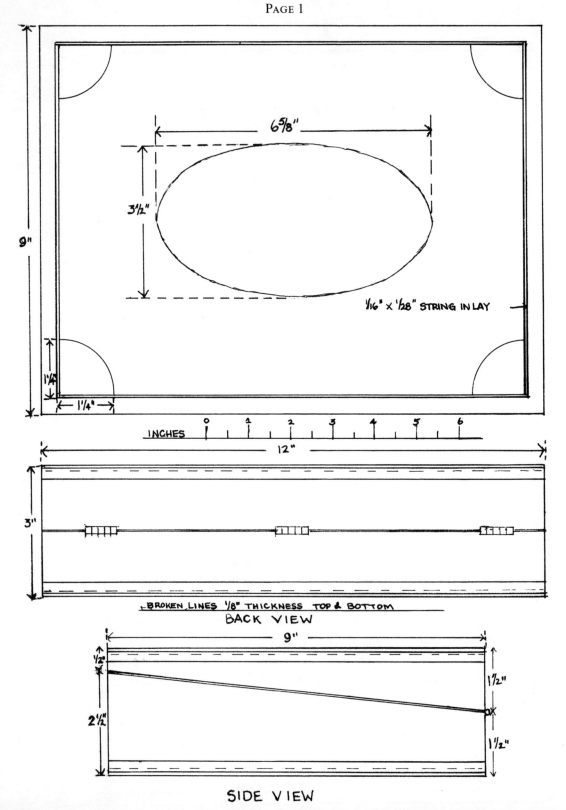

6⅝"

3½"

9"

1¼"

1¼"

¹⁄₁₆" x ¹⁄₂₈" STRING INLAY

INCHES

0 1 2 3 4 5 6

12"

3"

BROKEN LINES ⅛" THICKNESS TOP & BOTTOM

BACK VIEW

9"

½"

2½"

1½"

1½"

SIDE VIEW

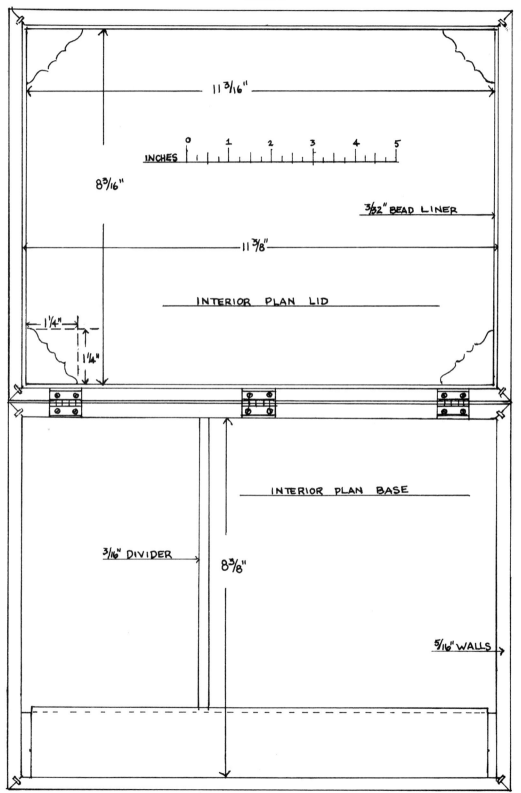

11 ³⁄₁₆"

INCHES 0 1 2 3 4 5

8 ³⁄₁₆"

³⁄₃₂" BEAD LINER

11 ³⁄₈"

INTERIOR PLAN LID

1 ¼"

1 ¼"

INTERIOR PLAN BASE

³⁄₁₆" DIVIDER

8 ³⁄₈"

⁵⁄₁₆" WALLS

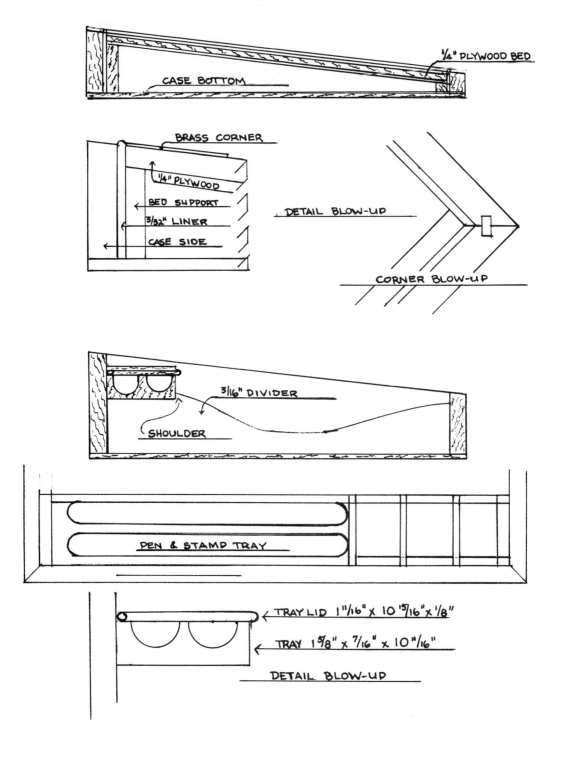

¼" PLYWOOD BED

CASE BOTTOM

BRASS CORNER

¼" PLYWOOD

BED SUPPORT

3/32" LINER

CASE SIDE

DETAIL BLOW-UP

CORNER BLOW-UP

3/16" DIVIDER

SHOULDER

PEN & STAMP TRAY

TRAY LID 1"/16" x 10 15/16" x ⅛"

TRAY 1⅝" x 7/16" x 10 11/16"

DETAIL BLOW-UP

following chapters are constructed in like manner but to avoid photo duplication, only this one illustrates corner construction.

A requisite common to these small boxes is the thickness or rather the thinness of the wood parts. Except for the top and bottom panels the narrow width parts can be re-sawed without later gluing.

A satisfying professional look will result when re-sawing the wood for all of these boxes if an 8″ fine tooth hollow ground saw is used. In fact, even cross cutting, mitering, and spline grooves can be done with practically no tearing.

So let's get started with the sides. Allowing an inch in length and ⅛″ in width for waste, cut one piece of stock 13-16″ thick x 2 15-16″ wide x 13″ long. Cut another 2 15-16″ wide x 10″ long. Since these wall pieces are the only ones to be 5-16″ thick, they can now be re-sawn to get two pieces from each length.

Tilt the fine tooth saw to 45°. Using the cross-cut gauge on the circular saw, square the wall pieces (12″ and 9″) on the 45° setting. Photo 1-1 shows the saw still tilted to 45° with the ripping fence set for the spline groove cut and saw blade raised to cut a groove depth of ⅛″ (saw cut width should not be more than 3-32″).

When making splines it takes very little more time to run five or six times the needed pieces for one box. Later, when making a similar box and using the same saw, identical splines will be needed.

Using 13-16″ waste wood, start with widths of not less than 3⅛″. Set ripping fence to cut ¼″ long. Using a pusher stick, cut 6 or more pieces 13-16″ thick, 3⅛″ wide, and ¼″ long. See photo 1-2.

Your saw throat plate probably has too wide a slot for the final spline cut. Find a thin (¼″ plywood will do) piece to drop over the saw after the ripping fence is set to slice splines to fit snugly into the prepared grooves. Have the plywood long enough to clamp on either front or rear of saw table. Lay the billet with the 13-16″ x 3⅛″ surface on the saw table, slice one trial piece which should measure 3⅛″ x ¼″—a snug fit. Make necessary fence adjustments and cut remaining splines.

Photos 1-3 and 1-4 show the next step. Taper a stick on one end to almost a sharp edge for applying glue to grooves. A small brush for half of spline, tap into groove, coat matching groove and both mitered surfaces, connect with hand pressure. Repeat with three other joints. A small strap clamp is ideal for this job; check with a square (photo 1-4).

After glue hardens overnight, smooth top and bottom surfaces. Photo 1-5

PHOTO 1-1

PHOTO 1-2

PHOTO 1-3

shows how pieces are re-sawed to be glued together to make up the required 9″ width. Glue edges and clamp for overnight setting. Smooth inside panel surfaces with plane or scraper so a uniform contact can be made with side wall surfaces. Panels should be oversize so exact positioning when gluing will be unnecessary. Glue side wall surfaces, place panels in position, place unit on saw table (or equivalent), cover the top panel with a flat piece of ¾″ plywood and press overnight with a 20 to 35-lb. weight. Hand plane top and bottom panel edges flush with the side walls. Rough sand all surfaces including top and bottom areas. The reason for sanding now is to remove all significant amounts of wood before routing for inlay.

Side wall inlay bands are the next operation. These ¼″ wide pieces are known as banding and may be chosen from a wide variety of patterns. Set the router fence so the ¼″ bit will make its channel less than ⅛″ from bottom and top edges. The object is to cover the glued joint with inlay (Photo 1-6). Rout to the depth of inlay thickness. Coat the inlay (not the channel) with glue on sides and bottom only; seat firmly with hammer; leave overnight. Rough sand these inlays so there will be no protrusions for the fence to ride against when working on the top.

Lengths of narrow inlay 1-16″ wide x 1-28″ thick are referred to as "strings." These should be ordered in holly (white wood) rather than satinwood (yellow). Change router bit to 1-16″, set fence to cut a channel ¼″ in from the edge of the top. Depth, of course, is the thickness of string inlay. Glue string, tap into groove with hammer; set overnight; rough sand before working the next step (photo 1-7).

Inlay for the top consists of a center oval and quarter fan corners. These pieces come to you in a veneer background which must be removed to the oval outline (photo 1-8). After the close saw cut, carefully remove what is left with hand tools (photo 1-9).

Turn the veneer over so that the paper side is up; mark crossed center lines (photo 1-10); and place to match center cross lines on box top. Hold firmly in place and outline with a needle point scriber. Hold the right angle lines of the corner pieces even with the string inlay on each corner and scribe the quarter circle. The resulting scratch lines are not very discernible so, before routing to depth, tap different number gouges with a mallet to deepen the lines. A ¼″ bit in the router will do very well for removing the wood to depth in both oval and corners (photos 1-11 and 1-12). Varying widths of #3 gouges are best for removing the thin line of wood remaining after routing (photo 1-13).

PHOTO 1-4

PHOTO 1-5

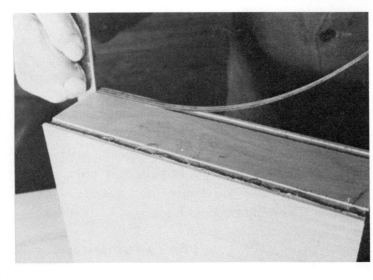

PHOTO 1-6

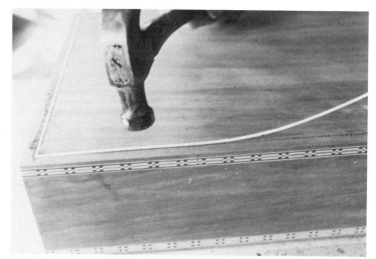

PHOTO 1-7

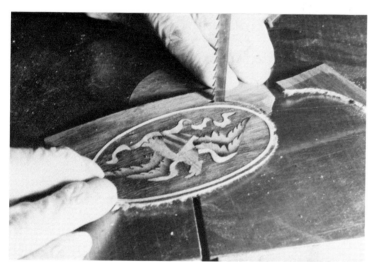

PHOTO 1-8

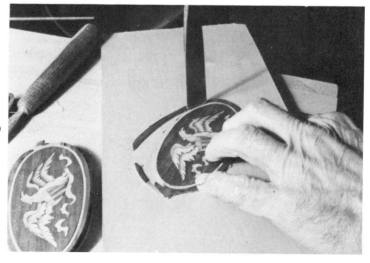

PHOTO 1-9

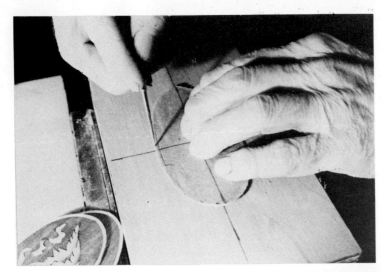

Photo 1–10

Photo 1–11

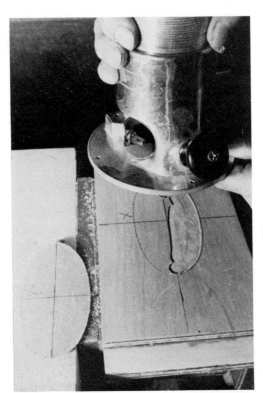

Photo 1–12

Seldom do oval inlays lie flat enough to remain exactly in position when they are covered with paper and a block for weighting. So to be safe, after coating with glue, place in position and, depending on size, press either one or two strips of masking tape to hold in position. Then place a piece of paper over veneer so glue will not adhere to unwanted surfaces. Next lay down a block close to the oval size and a weight (photo 1-14). Leave overnight.

Rough sand until flush with the top surface. As you cut the corner cavities, mark each piece and its corresponding corner, in case there is any variation in shape or size. Glue coat each piece; apply a strip of tape; cover with paper and a piece of ¾″ plywood larger than 9″ x 12″; and a weight.

Unless you are unusually skillful in the use of the belt sander, I advise sanding these inlays by hand. The risk of sanding through the thin inlay pieces is not worth the time saved. Rough sanding is always done with #60 grit.

Fine sand (#120 grit) the entire box, remembering that insufficient sanding will result in a poor final appearance after finish coatings have been applied.

The next step is to part the box into base and lid. Check with the line drawing (side view) to learn how a tapered board must be laid out so the resulting saw cut will leave a lid ½″ at the front and 1½″ at the back.

Start with a scrap piece say 3″ wide by 9″ for the taper plus about 2″ or 3″ on one end. (See photo 1-15.) The tapered board is alongside the fence with the narrow end pointing front (to the left) and is measured to hold the case bottom toward the fence (photo 1-16). Measure and mark the front end of jig from fence edge 1½″ out. Measure 9″ back and mark. This point is to be 2½″ from the fence out, leaving a ½″ shoulder to keep box in place.

Using the fine-tooth saw, raise it to cut a depth of ⅜″. With the lid facing out, saw one end. Turn jig end over end and cut the other end of box. Tilt the saw to about 3°, set fence to match end saw cuts first on the front long side, reset and saw the back. Smooth the resulting edges with a hand plane.

Set up the bench saw table with a ¾″ dado combination to recess for ¾″ narrow brass butts; depth of dado is to be ½ of closed hinge. Set fence for one inch to start of hinge cut (photo 1-17). Saw both ends of each 1½″ high on the long side. Set fence to center of 12″ side and run bottom and lid. Caution: keep matching ends of box to the fence. Fasten hinges in place.

Re-saw enough 3-32″ wood to line the lid walls. Miter corners and cut each piece 1-16″ higher than the wall around the top edge. Spot glue, place, and clamp (photo 1-18).

Photo 1-13

Photo 1-14

Photo 1-15

PHOTO 1–16

PHOTO 1–17

PHOTO 1–18

The pen and stamp tray does not have to follow the drawing too closely except that it must fit snugly. The tray can be started with a block 1⅛″ x 7-16″ x 10 11-16″. At one end saw three cross grooves about one inch apart, sized to receive ⅛″ strips to divide the stamp wells. The rest of the distance, cut two channels with a deep gouge for pens (photo 1-19). Also observe on this photograph a ¼″ thick block at each end of tray. These provide a receiving hole for the hinge pins which will be cut on the lid ends.

The tray lid can be 1 11-16″ wide, 10 15-16″ long, and ⅛″ thick. As the photo shows, this length is cut so that there is a ⅛″ square at the back to be rounded into a ⅛″ pin. This process is repeated on the other end. Round the back and front edges. Rough and fine sand all surfaces including the two end blocks. After boring pin holes, glue, place, and brad one end block. Insert the lid pin in this end. Glue other end block, place over lid pin and brad in place. This unit should be a snug fit in box. After trial, spot glue the back surface of the tray and clamp in place. If necessary remove hinges for clamping.

Make a 3-16″ divider strip to fit from front to back of box. At its highest point, it should be ⅛″ above bottom of tray. Cut that ⅛″ shoulder exactly the tray width from the back wall (drawing page 3). Glue bottom of strip, place in position, set overnight.

Prepare a ¼″ plywood writing bed to fit inside the top lid of the box. Measure accurately first the height of bed support blocks made of ¼″ plywood necessary to bring the writing bed in line with base box height at hinge side. Repeat with low or front side. Spot glue both bed supports in place and clamp in position on front and back walls.

Carefully look at and understand what has been done to the brass box corners (photo 1-20). The purchased box corner, shown on the right must be cut with tin snips so that it is not over ¼″ in height when applied to each corner (center and left of photo). Drill a screw hole in each right-angle surface, countersink that hole, place the brass piece on the corner of the plywood bed with one thickness of blotting paper under the brass fitting's top surface for clearance for later blotting paper insertion, screw in place. Coat the top surfaces of support pieces with plenty of glue; press writing bed in place (photo 1-21). Blotting paper (choice of color) is to be cut accurately and fitted after final finish is completed.

Finishing materials can now be applied according to instructions in Chapter 15.

PHOTO 1–19

PHOTO 1–20

PHOTO 1–21

2

Tissue Box

MATERIALS

2 walls 5-16″ x 2⅜″ x 11″
2 walls 5-16″ x 2⅜″ x 5½″
2 panels (top and bottom) 5¾″ x 11¼″ x ⅛″ thick

INLAY

¼″ banding 3-ft. lengths (2)

HARDWARE

¾″ narrow brass butt hinges (2)

THIS BOX is something one can do without, but then again, it is something very nice to have. I made six of them while preparing this chapter—two each of walnut, cherry, and mahogany. They all looked equally attractive.

The construction routine is like the Portable Desk. Process two walls 5-16″ x 2⅜″ x 11″ and two shorter walls 5-16″ x 2⅜″ x 5½″ (photo 1-3). Tilt fine tooth saw to 45°, square cut ends to exactly 11″ and 5½″. Follow Chapter 1 instructions for spline milling, glue assembly, and clamp (photo 1-4). Leveling surface, top and bottom of rectangle is essential for bonding top and bottom panels.

An 8″ fine tooth saw will not re-saw 5¾″ so two pieces will have to make up the width (photo 1-5). Before re-sawing 13-16″ wood, run each edge of every piece over the jointer for a good, square gluing surface. The ⅛″ top and bottom panels, after gluing, must be smooth surface for attachment to the sides.

Choose one panel for the top, mark for the slot (½″ x 8″), jigsaw this opening. Round the edge with stiff sand paper or a "sand stick," (described in

TISSUE BOX

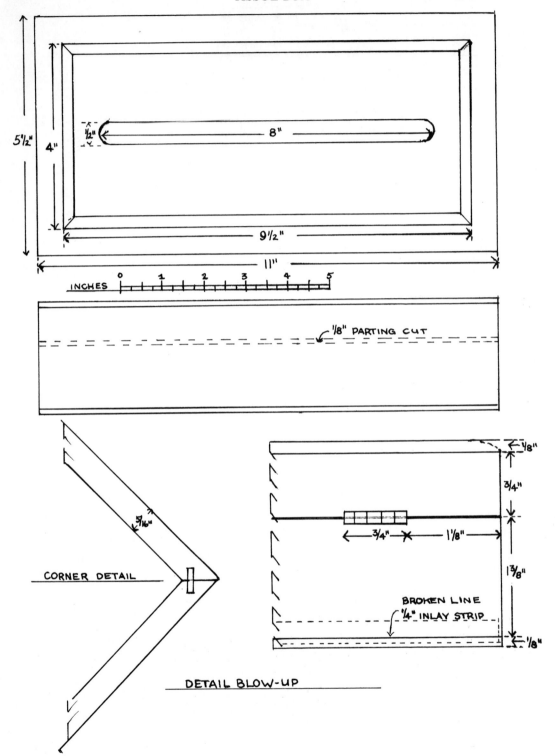

5½"
4"
½"
8"
9½"
11"

INCHES
0 1 2 3 4 5

⅛" PARTING CUT

CORNER DETAIL

5/16"

DETAIL BLOW-UP

⅛"
¾"
¾" 1⅛"
1⅜"
BROKEN LINE
¼" INLAY STRIP
⅛"

Photo 2–1

Photo 2–2

Photo 2–3

Photo 2-4

Photo 2-5

Chapter 15). Glue top and bottom wall surfaces with glue, position panels, place unit on level surface (saw table) with a ¾″ plywood piece on top of the top panel and weight with at least 20 pounds. Set overnight.

Rout lower sides for ¼″ banding, as discussed in Chapter 1. Rough sand all surfaces. Re-set router fence for a ¾″ border on the top (photo 2-1). Square out corners with hand chisels.

The next operation will be repeated many times throughout this book so a thorough description of the process is in order.

The ends of the ¼″ strips must be mitered, so a simple special miter box is needed. Provide a ¾″ piece of plywood about 3″ wide x 8″ long and a piece of ¼″ plywood about 1½″ wide x 8″ long. Glue and brad the thin piece on the ¾″ bed along the back edge (keep the brads away from the center which will have the miter cuts). Using a combination square, carefully mark first a right then a left 45° miter line, spaced about ½″ apart. Between the two, a 90° cut may be needed occasionally. Your bench tools should include a really fine tooth saw that can be purchased at any hobby shop. Use this saw with precision to cut through the ¼″ thickness on each line. When making these guide cuts and also when in use, hold the ¾″ base block securely in a bench vise keeping the working surface above the vise jaws.

Hold a length of banding against the fence and flat on the bed surface; miter the end. Hold the banding strip over a channel with the mitered tip at the end of groove. Mark the strip carefully at opposite end, place in miter box, and cut to the mark. Glue bottom and edges of strip, place in groove, tap firmly in place with a hammer. Continue around the other three sides (photo 2-1).

If you have had enough experience with a portable belt sander, one may be used to rough sand the top (photo 2-2), otherwise hand sand. Using a small block plane, make a long tapered round on the top edge (photo 2-3). Since there is no inlay to cover the top joint, plane this round down close to the joint so very little end wood will show. Rough sand these rounded surfaces. Fine sand all surfaces. Using the fine tooth saw, set the fence to part the box into 1½″ bottom which will leave a one inch top (photo 2-4). Smooth the sawed surfaces. Set up the ¾″ dado head and follow this operation described in Chapter 1 (photo 2-5). Fasten the hinges. Fold a piece of #120 grit paper and blunt all right-angle sharp corners. Finish according to instructions in Chapter 15.

3

Playing Card Box

MATERIALS

    2 walls 5-16″ x 2″ x 7½″

    2 walls 5-16″ x 2″ x 4½″

    2 panels (top and bottom) ⅛″ x 4¾″ wide x 7¾″ long

    enough 3-32″ thick wood for lid pocket and card deck platforms

    enough 1-16″ wood for base liner

INLAY

    ¼″ banding 3-ft. lengths (2)

    4″ x 2″ eagle oval (1)

HARDWARE

    ¾″ narrow brass butt hinges (2)

WHEN YOU HAVE two tables for bridge wouldn't it be pleasant to just walk over to the coffee table, pick up a box and find two decks, two score pads, and two pencils? All that, after you have had the satisfaction of making the box.

The procedure for making this box is a carbon copy of the two preceding pieces. The top and bottom banding on the sides covers the joints as on the Portable Desk (photo 1-6). Rough sanding at this point is indicated on the top if there is much wood removal needed for a smooth surface to inlay.

Procedural instructions will be repeated to accompany the photos for oval inlaying. Photo 1-8 shows veneer being removed by band saw close to the string outline. Photo 1-9 shows how to trim the remainder of background from the outline.

PLAYING CARD BOX
PAGE 1

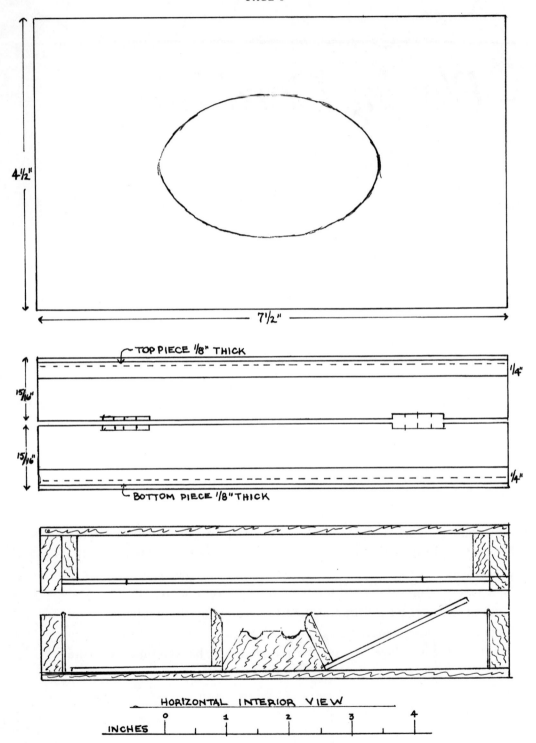

4½"

7½"

TOP PIECE ⅛" THICK

¼"

15/16"

15/16"

¼"

BOTTOM PIECE ⅛" THICK

HORIZONTAL INTERIOR VIEW

INCHES
0   1   2   3   4

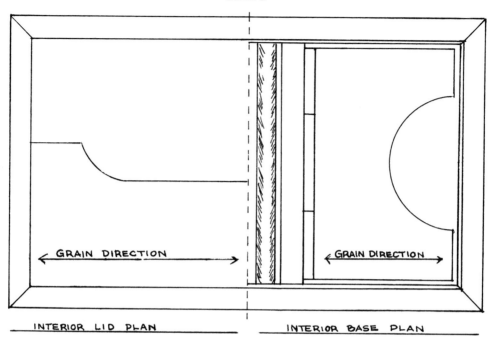

INTERIOR LID PLAN | INTERIOR BASE PLAN

GRAIN DIRECTION

GRAIN DIRECTION

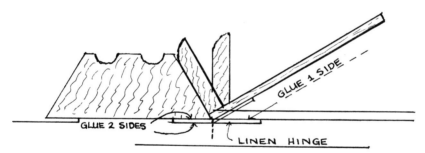

GLUE 1 SIDE

GLUE 2 SIDES

LINEN HINGE

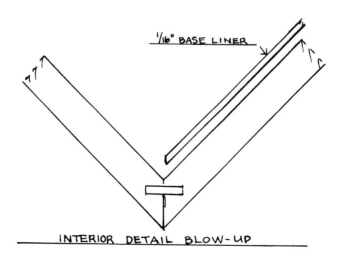

1/16" BASE LINER

INTERIOR DETAIL BLOW-UP

Ovals are backed up with brown paper to keep all the design pieces in place as a unit. This paper backing must be uppermost when inlaying; otherwise the paper would be between two layers of glue which would prevent good bonding of wood to wood. Photo 1-10 illustrates how the oval is centered and balanced from end to end. Draw a pencil line lengthwise down the center of the oval with a right-angle line across. These lines are placed over corresponding lines on the box top. Hold firmly in place, scribe a line around the oval, and proceed with either the router or by deepening the scribed line with #3 and #4 gouges. This hand tool operation is necessary whether or not it is done before the routing. When it precedes the routing, a much more discernible line can be followed with the router (photo 1-12).

Waste wood must be trimmed inside the oval line (photo 1-13). Probably there will be areas where a slight shave of wood must come off so the oval will fit neatly in place. A good habit to acquire when inlaying ovals is to mark an X on one end of the oval and a matching one on the box top. That prevents the oval from being turned end for end.

As photo 1-14 shows, coat the oval recess with glue, fit inlay in place accurately, using one piece of masking tape to hold the oval from shifting. Cover with one piece of paper to prevent any overflow glue from adhering to unwanted surfaces. Cover the paper with an oval piece of scrap lumber sawn slightly larger than the inlay. Be sure the covering wood is evenly placed over the oval and weight with 20 to 30 pounds. Set overnight. Rough sand (60 grit) with either the belt sander or by hand. Fine sand for a surface acceptable for finishing materials (photo 3-1).

Use the fine tooth saw raised to about ⅜″ in height, set the fence to part the box exactly in half (15-16″ bottom, 15-16″ top) and smooth these sawed edges with sand paper (photo 3-2). Next comes the ¾″ dado routine for hinge cut-outs explained in Chapter 1 (photo 1-17). Fasten hinges with screws.

Measure inside height of box bottom half, add 1-16″, and re-saw enough wood for the side liners. Miter ends for a neat fit. Spot glue, slide in place, and set overnight (photo 3-3). Line drawing horizontal interior view shows in detail functional parts to be made. Also the line drawing blow-up illustrates even more details.

PHOTO 3–1

PHOTO 3–2

PHOTO 3-3

First the center block 1⅛″ wide by ½″ high by inside box measurement from front to back. Angle the sides, leaving 11-16″ top surface for pencil grooves. Cut pencil channels with a hand gouge #11.

Re-saw wood to 3-32″ thick for linen hinged card deck platform and lid score-card pocket. See line drawing. First cut the card deck platforms to size. These will measure ⅛″ less in width than the inside box width. Length will be determined in this manner: total inside box length, less 1⅛″ center block. The result should then be divided by two less another ⅛″ for clearance on each piece. Saw the half round finger clearance. Sand and round edges, final sand top surfaces. Size vertical pincer pieces to 3-16″ thick by ¾″ high by length to match deck platform width. Round top edges as shown on line drawing. Coat bottom edges with glue and line evenly with ends of platforms, press, and leave overnight.

Cut two pieces of linen for hinges about 1″ x 3½″. On a working surface, lay a piece of paper so that when coated with glue the linen will not adhere to an unwanted surface. Coat with glue the upper surface of the linen pieces and place the center block over one half of each linen piece. Now the platforms are butted up to the center block (see line drawing blow-up). After overnight setting, carefully coat with glue only the linen under the center block. Center the whole unit in the box, being sure neither platform scrapes the box sides when raised (photo 3-3). Press for good contact.

To form a pocket in the lid, cut to fit in length a piece of 3-32″ re-sawed wood 2¼″ wide. Cove cut for appearance, round cove edge, sand outside surface. A support piece at each end (line drawing) sized to ¼″ x ½″ x 2″ long should be spot glued to end wall. Spot glue top surface to support pieces, press in place the thin cove panel.

Feel over all edges and, where necessary, sand sharp right-angle edges with folded #120 grit paper. Examine the entire box for any overlooked blemishes. The box is now ready for the application of finishing materials. Read Chapter 15 to familiarize yourself with all aspects of the finishing process.

4

Sewing Table

MATERIALS

    4 legs 1¼″ x 1¼″ x 25½″ long

    3 panels 2 side, 1 back 13-16″ thick, 12″ wide, 10″ long

    1 top panel ⅝″ x 15″ x 15″ long

    2 leaf panels ⅝″ x 10″ x 15″ long

    4 division strips ⅝″ x 1¼″ x 13″ long

    drawer front wood ⅝″ x 10″ x 12″ long

    4 sq. ft. poplar re-sawed to 5-16″ for drawer sides and backs

    5 sq. ft. poplar re-sawed to ¼″ for drawer bottoms and tray

    3 lengths 3-16″ dowel rods

INLAY

    2 bell flower leg drops

    4 lengths ¼″ banding

    5 lengths 1-16″ string

HARDWARE

    drop leaf hinges (4)

    drawer handles (drop pulls) (3)

DRESSMAKING AND NEEDLEWORK of all kinds have always been popular. Even today their adherents are legion. The combination of utility and a beautiful piece of furniture for any room in the house is unbeatable. For the sake of variety, this table was made of cherry. Walnut and mahogany are also good.

SEWING TABLE
Page 1

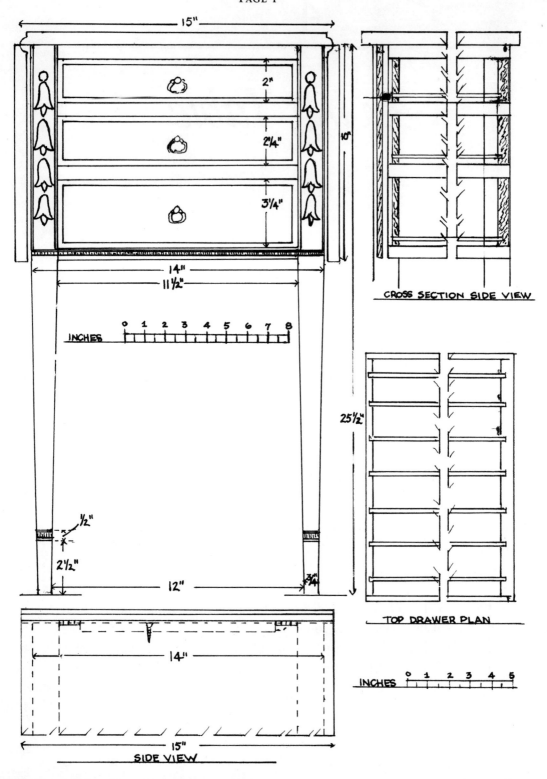

CROSS SECTION SIDE VIEW

TOP DRAWER PLAN

SIDE VIEW

INCHES 0 1 2 3 4 5 6 7 8

INCHES 0 1 2 3 4 5

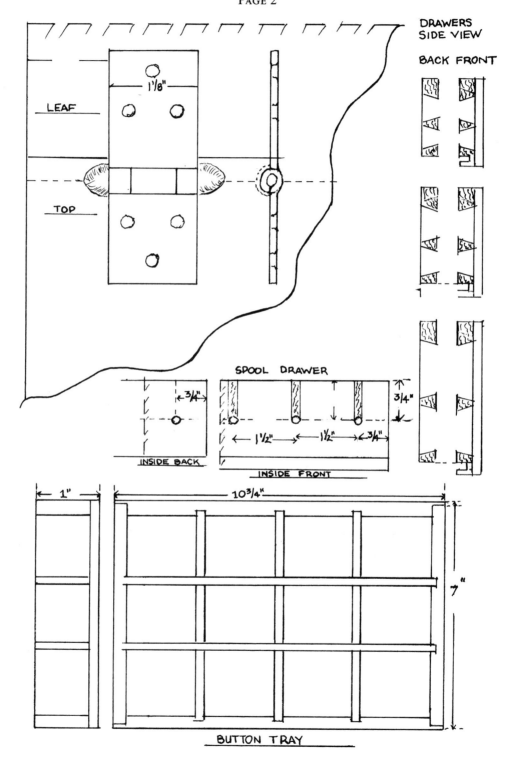

DRAWERS
SIDE VIEW

BACK FRONT

LEAF

1⅛"

TOP

SPOOL DRAWER

¾"

¾"

INSIDE BACK

1½"   1½"   ¾"

INSIDE FRONT

1"

10¾"

7"

BUTTON TRAY

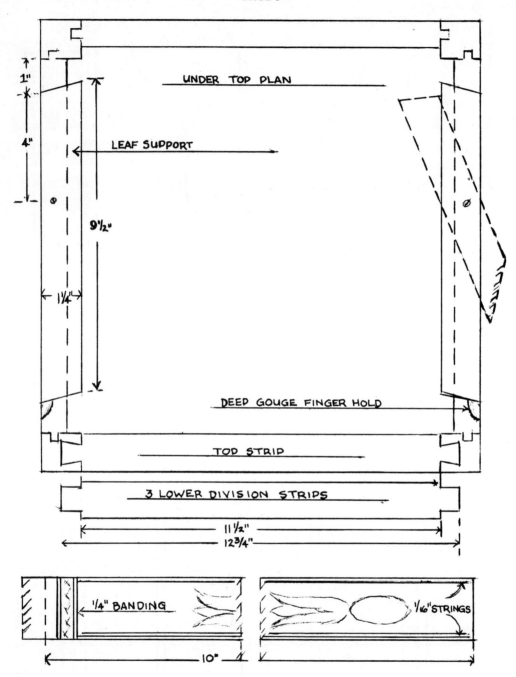

UNDER TOP PLAN

LEAF SUPPORT

1"

4"

9½"

1¼"

DEEP GOUGE FINGER HOLD

TOP STRIP

3 LOWER DIVISION STRIPS

11½"

12¾"

¼" BANDING

¹⁄₁₆" STRINGS

10"

Start by sizing the four legs. Rough cut 26½″ long. Rip to 1 5-16″ x 1 5-16″, make a light (3-32″) jointer cut on all 4 sides of each piece to remove saw marks. Saw to exact 25½″ length. Glue together pieces of 13-16″ wood to make up 2 case sides and 1 back. All three are the same finished size: 12″ long (horizontal) and 10″ wide (vertical); after joining together, cut to finished size. Even out all surface glue joints either by hand or belt sander.

The two 10″ sides of each panel will be joined to the legs but since the grain of the legs is vertical and the panels horizontal, good construction calls for ¼″ x ¼″ tongues cut on these 10″ sides (photo 4-1 and line drawing). Mount the dado side cutters on the mandrel with a ¼″ spacer washer between; raise the cutters to ¼″ height. Set the fence so the planned ¼″ tongue will leave a 5-16″ shoulder from the front surface; cut these tongues the full 10″ length.

Change to the fine tooth saw, set fence to remove waste shoulder wood on front corners, then on the back corners. Choose which 12″ sides will be for the bottom edges, using the bandsaw, and cut the ¼″ tongues on a rough dado radius at the bottom end for clearance in the receiving leg grooves.

Probably it will be well at this point to explain the difference between tongue and groove joints and mortise and tenon. Tongue and groove means the groove ends are open whereas a mortise has square cut closed ends to receive tenons that have been cut to fit. An illustration of a mortise is photo 4-2.

The top 12″ edge of side panels can be cut for leaf supports. These pieces must not be thicker than the top front strip; otherwise when the support is extended, it would not clear the drawer side. Cut-outs are angled on the ends so the supports will stop without turning too far (line drawing and photo 4-3).

Returning to the leg blanks, it can be seen on line drawing (under top plan) on which sides of the four legs the ¼″ x ¼″ grooves must be milled. Set up the two dado side cutters to plow the ¼″ grooves to a depth of ¼″. Measure accurately the front shoulders of panels, set the fence to that measurement for groove cutting. Six grooves must be cut and since they are what might be called pairs, the front corner must be held against the fence for each cut which means that three gooves will be started on the saw at the top and the other three must be dropped onto the dado at the bottom end and pushed through to the top. To be sure these grooves are being milled on the right sides and corners, stand the four legs upright, hold together, and mark a rough groove line where each is to be cut.

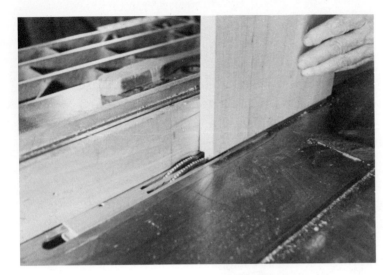

PHOTO 4-1

PHOTO 4-2

PHOTO 4-3

Also mark the leg tops B for back surface, S for outside, and F for front. Be careful; it is no fun to waste a leg blank. The side panels are 10″ high so grooves must radius out at 9¾″.

Cut division strip mortises next. It is much less confusing and simplifies figuring if the tenons are planned for the bottom of each strip. That means there will be only one shoulder measurement to remember when laying off the mortises for each drawer height (photo 4-2). The same position and size tenons are to be milled on the top strip which will later have the dovetail shape cut on each end (line drawing and photo 4-3).

Division strips are to be ⅝″ thick, 1¼″ wide, and 11½″ long between shoulders. Tenons are to be ¼″ x 1¼″ x ¾″ long with 3-16″ shoulders cut on front and back edges (photo 4-3). By making the division strips now, both tenons and mortises can be worked and fitted to complete that operation. Choose one division strip for the bottom and, along the full length of front surface, rout out a ¼″ wide groove for banding inlay ⅛″ up from the bottom corner (photo 4-4). This must be done before proceeding with the legs so the strip can be inserted into its mortises to line up the inlay groove across the legs (photos 4-2 and 4-4) which must be cut in by hand using a fine tooth back saw and a narrow chisel for cleaning out.

Next, mount the 1-16″ bit in router to a depth of 1-28″ for string inlay. Set the fence to cut 3-32″ in from the front edges, run these grooves up from the ¼″ banding groove right through the top end (photo 4-2).

Now the drawing calls for a taper on all four legs. This is not a complicated operation when you understand what is to be accomplished and since it will be repeated a number of times throughout this book, a detailed description of the process is in order. First determine the difference in measurement between the full size of the leg and the proposed lower end dimension. In this case the legs are tapered from 1¼″ down to ¾″—a difference of ½″, which means ¼″ on each side. Set the jointer depth to ⅛″. Mark the front (toward you) jointer bed at a point that will allow the lowered leg to start a tapered cut 1″ below the 10″ side panel line. Lowering the leg onto the jointer results in the cut starting at nothing and ending at the ⅛″ depth when passed to the leg end. Another pass is necessary on this same side to gain the ¼″ desired depth. *But* to keep from ending up with an unwanted starting trough, start this second cut 1″ below the first. Repeat on the three other surfaces and all around on the remaining legs.

Mount the ½″ dado cutters and set to the depth of ½″ banding inlay thickness. Set fence so the cut will start at 2½″ up from the bottom of legs. Using the cross cut gauge, pass each leg surface over the dado for the ankle band. When cutting the ½″ inlay for ankle bands, make each piece slightly more than ¾″. The most convenient method for cutting these small pieces is to use the small miter box made for the tissue project, Chapter 2. Use the 90° saw cut, pencil mark a point that will result in the banding length desired, cut 16 pieces. These may now be glued in place. To start gluing, place one dry piece in a groove for the next one to butt against. Glue the second one, press in place against the first, remove the dry one and continue with the glued pieces, butting each against the prior one. Do all four legs in like manner.

The string inlay should be glued in place next. This is done before the ¼″ banding is placed across the leg because it is easier to cut the excess string on the banding line than to butt up to previously glued band inlay. Now follow with the band across the leg; set overnight (photo 4-2).

Two leg drops to be inlaid in the front surfaces of the front legs are imbedded in extra large background veneer. These panels will be cut accurately to fit the recess routed out between the strings and cross band. Using a ¼″ router bit, set to veneer depth and cut close to previously glued inlay right through the top end. With a ¾″ or larger chisel, clean out the wood up to the inlay. The leg drop panels may be cut very close to size with heavy duty scissors. For final fitting, rub with a sandpaper-covered block. Coat the panels with glue (paper side up) place in position and, if necessary, tape to hold in place, then cover with a piece of paper. Do this to both legs. Place the glued surfaces face to face, being sure there are 2 sheets of paper between, C clamp them together, and set overnight. Rough and fine sand all surfaces on the four legs (photo 4-5).

Glue the ¼″ banding inlay in the bottom strip channel; after setting trim to the shoulders, rough sand all four strip face surfaces.

After checking the tongues and grooves for fit, assemble the case sides by coating a tongue and its groove with glue; press together by hand keeping leg top and side panel top edge even. Repeat with the back leg. Pull up to a tight fit with two bar clamps. Repeat with the other side unit, and set overnight. Repeat glue coating routine with the back panel. The front strips must be glued the same way with the only difference being the mortises instead of grooves. If the bar clamps

Photo 4–4

Photo 4–5

Photo 4–6

are left tightened on the sides, there will be more area to angle the next set for squaring the case. This next set of clamps is to be placed over the ones drawing up the sides; when tightened, front and back joints will be tight. Hold a large square on the case to see if any adjustment is necessary. Should this be so, shift the last placed clamps off parallel with the case line. When tightened again the case may be farther out of square; if so, shift the clamps the other way. Place the top strip in position with the shoulders down for overnight setting.

If the dovetail shape has not been cut on strip ends, do it at this time (photos 4-3 and 4-6). Place in position, scribe an outline around each end. There will probably be a variation in the shape and size of these two tails so mark one end for proper placement when glued in permanently. Use a ¼″ router bit set to the depth of the shoulders, rout and trim out with hand tools to the scribed lines, glue the cut-outs and tails, seat in place and, for extra strength, drive a 1″ nail into each tail.

Drawer runners are the next pieces to make. Any kind of wood will do if it is large enough to get pieces 1⅛″ wide by 1¼″ high by 11″ long. Six pieces are required. One corner must be sawed out to leave an L shape ⅝″ on the bottom and about 7-16″ on the upright leg. 7-16″ should be the distance from the inside leg surface to the side panel surface. Bore and countersink for two attachment screws (photo 4-4).

Front strips, side and back panels were measured and milled to be flush with the leg surfaces. If there is any variation, a hand plane will even out the difference. Rough and fine sand all these surfaces.

Mill the support pieces to fit side panel cut-outs (photo 4-7 and line drawing). A screw hole must be bored about 4″ from the back end and, as will be observed on drawing, off center in width because these 1¼″ wide strips are to be flush on the outside. The holes should be bored and countersunk ⅜″ from the outside edge. Find and note on the line drawing the Deep Gouge Finger Hold. These are a convenience when swinging out the supports (see drawing, pg. 34).

Measure the openings for drawers—height, width and depth—which should be from the front surface to the inside corner of the back legs. These small drawers should have ⅝″ thick fronts of case wood and 5-16″ sides, backs, and bottoms of poplar which is commonly used for interior parts because it is easier to work than the harder case woods. There are drawers in a number of projects in

Photo 4–7

Photo 4–9

Photo 4–10

this book and Chapter 14 on dovetailing deals in depth with all related furniture parts calling for this joint, so to avoid duplication, please refer to that chapter for complete drawer making.

Before assembling the top drawer, follow the line drawing for spool rod holes in the back and corresponding slots in the front piece.

The middle drawer has a button tray with a suggested size: 6½″ from front to back, 1⅜″ height by the inside drawer width in length. For sides and division, use ¼″ thick poplar. ⅛″ thick bottom panel fastened to sides with glue and brads. Division strips must be made like a honeycomb to fit inside the drawer. Cut slots in the bottom half in height where the cross pieces will fit and slot the top half of cross pieces so all pieces slip in place, making a single unit (photo 4-9). The corners of the four-sided box can be any kind of a joint desired, even dovetail if you have that much ambition.

Choose from your stock of 13-16″ wood one or more boards to make up the top and two drop leaves. Presumably you do not have a surface planer so have this lumber dressed to ⅝″ thickness, cross cut enough pieces 16″ long to provide a top 15″ x 15″ and two leaves 15″ long by 10″ wide. Run all 15″ edges over the jointer for good glue joints. Adjust 3 bar clamps for each panel, glue edges and clamp, keeping the board surfaces even with each other, and set overnight. Rough sand all panel surfaces.

Before sawing the panels to length, rout out and fit the drop leaf hinges. This is an exacting operation to make the leaf drop as it should without binding or swinging too far away from the special molding worked on the top. The router bit should be set to a depth slightly more than the thickness of the hinge steel. Note line drawing for this chapter as well as the drawing for Chapter 8 and photo 4-10. These hinges are designed for table leaves, having one long side and a short one, also the pin roll is not all on one side of the hinge. When positioned and fitted properly, dropping the leaf will make it follow the thumbnail molding evenly to its lowered position.

Cut the quarter round rolls on the top edges according to the drawing for Chapter 8 with a matching cove on each leaf. Sand these molded edges. Place together the three panels upside down (these panels are still oversize). Carefully place hinge 1″ in from the proposed finished end, line up hinge pin 5-16″ in from the molded edge of top panel (short flap of hinge fastened to top). Scribe hinge outline, rout out close to line, finish with hand tools. Use a 5-16″ #11 gouge to

PHOTO 4–11   PHOTO 4–12

channel out for the hinge roll (photo 4-10). In case an adjustment is necessary in hinge position, just finish and attach the first hinge to check, then follow with three more. The top is now in a three-part unit. Place a straight edge along the proposed front line, pencil mark, band saw, and finish with a jointer cut to smooth out the final line. Set saw fence to 15″, run the unit for a straight back line, finish with a jointer cut.

Lay the top unit right side up with leaves extended, hand plane any variation where top meets leaves, rough sand. Still keeping the leaves intact, perform the ¼″ banding routine, setting the router fence to cut about ⅜″ in from the edge. Miter banding inlay but do not cut where leaf meets top, continue all the way around, glue inlay, set overnight. Use fine tooth saw for parting inlay between leaves and top, sand to a smooth finished edge. Finish sand under side of leaves and rough and finish sand entire top surface, also the ⅝″ edge all around (photo 4-11).

Bore top attachment screw holes in the case—four to be bored on an angle close to legs in the side pieces and one about center of back. Also a countersunk hole about center of front top strip. Attach top. For completed table, see photo 4-12 and for finishing instructions, see Chapter 15.

SEWING TABLE   43

5

Tilt-Top Tables

MATERIALS

top A ⅝″ x 17″ x 21″ long
top B ⅝″ x 13¾″ x 17¾″
post A 2⅜″ Dia., 19½″ long
post B 2¼″ Dia., 18½″ long
wood for legs A 1″ thick
wood for legs B 13-16″ thick
wood for hinge blocks A and B 13-16″
wood for battens ¾″

INLAY

oval 6″ x 9″ (1)
oval 5″ x 8″ (1)
lengths of 1-16″ string (2)

HARDWARE

table catches (2)

THESE TABLES take another design direction. Down through the years, furniture styles change but there are a few basic forms that seem to survive each passing fad. Tripods, as with most of the furniture pictured and described here, never go out of style.

The posts can be completely turned before further work is done on them. Because the tables are similar the instructions will assume only one is being built.

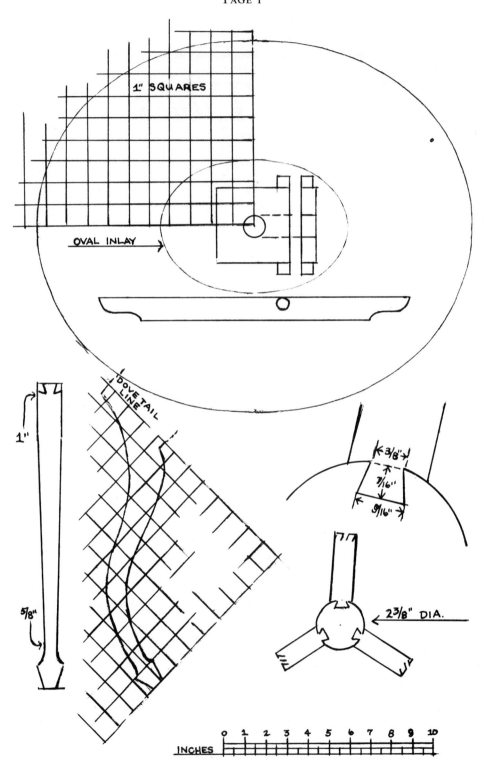

1" SQUARES

OVAL INLAY

DOVETAIL LINE

1"

5/8"

3/8"

7/16"

9/16"

2 3/8" DIA.

INCHES
0 1 2 3 4 5 6 7 8 9 10

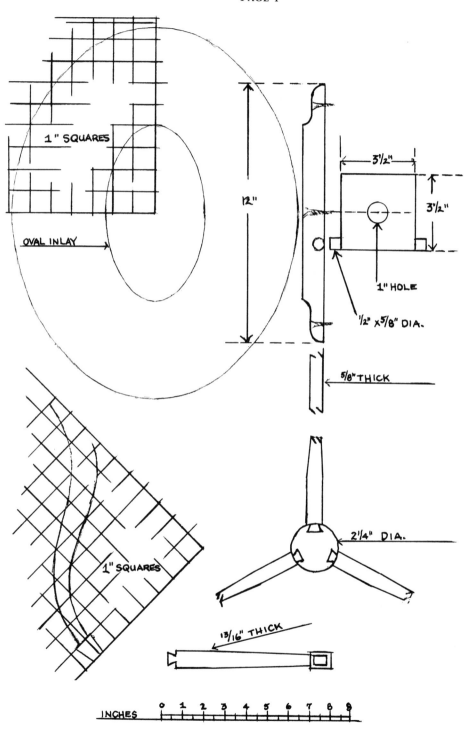

1" SQUARES

OVAL INLAY

12"

3½"

3½"

1" HOLE

½" x ⅝" DIA.

⅝" THICK

1" SQUARES

2¼" DIA.

13/16" THICK

INCHES   0 1 2 3 4 5 6 7 8 9

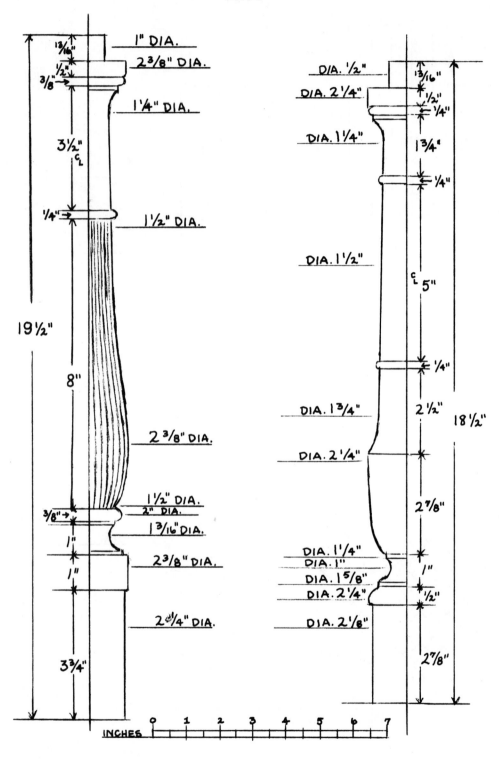

1" DIA.

2³⁄₈" DIA.

1¹⁄₄" DIA.

1¹⁄₂" DIA.

2³⁄₈" DIA.

1¹⁄₂" DIA.
2" DIA.
1³⁄₁₆" DIA.

2³⁄₈" DIA.

2¹⁄₄" DIA.

¹³⁄₁₆"
¹⁄₂"
³⁄₈"

3¹⁄₂"
c_L

¹⁄₄"

19¹⁄₂"

8"

³⁄₈"→
1"
1"

3³⁄₄"

DIA. ¹⁄₂"

DIA. 2¹⁄₄"

DIA. 1¹⁄₄"

DIA. 1¹⁄₂"

DIA. 1³⁄₄"

DIA. 2¹⁄₄"

DIA. 1¹⁄₄"
DIA. 1"
DIA. 1⁵⁄₈"
DIA. 2¹⁄₄"

DIA. 2¹⁄₈"

¹³⁄₁₆"
¹⁄₂"
¹⁄₄"

1³⁄₄"

¹⁄₄"

c_L 5"

¹⁄₄"

2¹⁄₂"

2⁷⁄₈"

1"
¹⁄₂"

2⁷⁄₈"

18¹⁄₂"

INCHES

0 1 2 3 4 5 6 7

Cut post A to finished size 2⅜″ x 2⅜″ x 19½″ long. Accurately mark the center of post ends. Sink an awl in these marks for lathe centers.

If this piece is well balanced, the lathe speed can be stepped up to about 1,750 RPM which will make turning smoother. If vibration is excessive, reduce speed. Using a large gouge, turn down to the full round (no flats remaining). Post A drawing shows diameters and longitudinal measurements of which only one must be accurate: the distance from the post bottom to the shoulder must measure the same as the dovetail line on the leg pattern.

The simplest and least expensive way to learn turning is by procuring any kind of cheap wood to make six or more posts about the size of post A. Be sure your turning tools are as sharp as you can make them, center a blank in the lathe, have post drawing A handy and wade in. After you spoil maybe five of them I'll bet the sixth will look pretty good. Now take a chance on the good wood post you want to use. There is one good thing going for you: only one of a kind (photos 5-1 and 5-2).

Post A has 26 fine reeds for decoration. Your shop equipment should include an adjustable jig with interchangeable index heads (photo 5-3). I believe many amateur shops would have various attachments for router or drill press to do this kind of work, so the jig design would be governed by that equipment.

Designers of production furniture would draw this post to have a depressed curve at each end of the reeds so the bit can cut through without hand work. The comparative appearance of this turning is well worth the extra time involved. Leave the post mounted in the jig to finish reed shaping with a V carving tool and a ¼″ #3 gouge (photo 5-4). Finish sand reeds.

To divide the post circumference into three parts, set a pair of dividers to the radius (photo 5-5). Make slight adjustment if necessary. Scribe a deep scratch line down the side of the post to the shoulder at each division point (photo 5-6). The post is now put aside until work on the legs reaches a point where a suitable angle can be determined for cutting the dovetail shoulder.

Make a leg pattern for table A of hard cardboard or other suitable material by laying it off in one-inch square blocks (table A drawing). Pencil in the leg shape, cut to outline. On one-inch thick leg wood, outline the pattern and, possibly, depending on the width of board, nesting the next two can save material. Bandsaw the legs (photo 5-7).

Photo 5-1

Photo 5-2A

Photo 5-2B

Photo 5–3

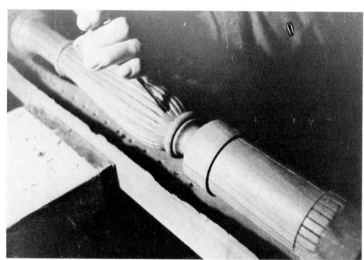

Photo 5–4

Photo 5–5

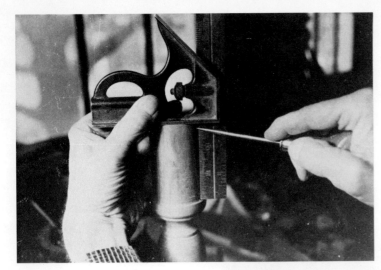

Photo 5-6

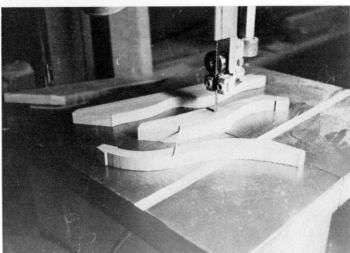

Photo 5-7

Photo 5-8

Using the dovetail drawing blow-up as a guide, tilt the fine tooth 8″ saw to an angle that will correspond to the drawing. Raise the saw to 7-16″ in height. Adjust the fence so a cut on each side of the leg will leave a dovetail shape about the size of the drawing (photo 5-8). Run all three legs over that set-up. To get the best angle for the shoulder cut, observe photo 5-5 again. Place the post, bottom up, in the vise, take one leg and pencil mark a line about ¼″ in from the straight edge on each side. Hold the leg upside down on the post bottom surface, positioning it to bring the ¼″ marks in line with the post radius, hold steady and follow the radius with a pencil, marking the top surface of the leg. This will show what angle to use for the shoulder cut. When made, this cut will be on a straight line, but since it should match the post radius, a #4 gouge can be used to cut the curve (photo 5-9).

To taper the leg from 1″ thick down to ⅝″ at the ankle, set the jointer depth of cut to 3-16″ and lower a leg onto the jointer bed at a point about 1″ from the bottom of dovetail (photo 5-10). Slowly push it forward until the cutting radius comes close to the spade foot top. Repeat on each leg side. To finish making the desired curve at the space foot top and tapering the foot itself, band saw as shown in photo 5-11.

Work on the post may be resumed. The three deep scratch division lines are guides for a ⅜″ machine bit spur. Because this bored surface is not full diameter, it must rest on a raised bed to stay parallel with the drill press bed and also the fence. Photo 5-12 shows two pieces of ¼″ scrap plywood nailed together to form a right-angle. The fence must be set to exactly one half of the diameter where post is to be bored. This measurement will include the ¼″ plywood. Set the drill bit to ½″ in depth and bore a line of holes as shown in photos 5-12 and 5-13.

The post must now be gripped firmly in the vise. To do this, use two pieces of ¼″ scrap plywood nailed to supporting blocks for the vise (photos 5-13 and 5-14). Incidentally the post shown in photo 5-14 is for table B.

To shape the dovetail socket, start by chopping straight down to remove the bored hole radii with a ¾″ chisel. Now that you have two straight side walls approximately the width of the small end of the dovetail, tilt the chisel to about the desired angle, chop down and clean out with a narrower chisel horizontally from the bottom end. Try fit again and again, gradually removing wood where necessary.

Photo 5-9

Photo 5-10

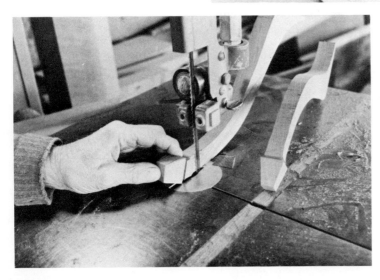

Photo 5-11

Photo 5–12

Photo 5–13

Photo 5–14

To prepare the legs up to and including the final sanding, the use of a sharp spoke shave will considerably cut sanding time. Before sanding, crown the top edge of the legs for a more finished and pleasing look. Rough and fine sand legs, coat sockets and tails with glue, enter and tap in place, stand upside down over night.

Make the hinge block for the post top next. Start with a 3½″ x 4½″ x 13-16″ piece, and mark the exact center for a 1″ hole. Bore the hole on the drill press for true vertical direction. Set the saw fence to cut ½″ to the outside of the blade. Cut down the 4″ sides, leaving enough wood to shape a ⅝″ diameter dowel ½″ long on each end; finish cutting the straight line to the ⅝″ mark with the band saw. Choose a top corner for the dowel end and hand plane a ¼″ radius the full length. This forms ¼ of the ⅝″ dowels. Shape the rest of the rounds with hand tools, rough and fine sand all surfaces. Mark and cut in the table catch strike plate (flush on both right-angle surfaces).

Make a band saw cut the length of the post top dowel for a wedge. These wedge cuts should always be directioned so that when the block is placed properly, the saw cut will be at right-angles to the wood grain. For best appearance, one leg should come to the front when the top is tilted, so the block must have the dowel end lined at right angles to the front leg, which also calls for the wedge saw cut to line up with the front leg. Glue the 1″ hole sides (but not the pin) seat firmly, drive in a prepared wedge, chisel flush when set, sand.

Drawing A calls for a top board ⅝″ thick by 17″ wide by 21″ long. Depending on the available planing equipment, 13-16″ pieces can be either planed separately or glued up and planed as an oversize panel, rough sanded both sides.

A piece of heavy cardboard can be used to make the oval top pattern. Draw a longitudinal center line and a right-angle cross center line dividing the pattern board into quarters. Lay off one quarter into 1″ squares (line drawing) following the oval outline segment. Carefully cut to the line with scissors and, on the waste piece, cut to the extended center lines for a true quarter of the oval. Turn the waste piece over and also end for end to mark the adjoining quarter; repeat on the other half. It is well to preserve these quarter section marks and transfer them to the wood when marking the top. Cut to outline with scissors, place pattern on top board and outline in pencil. Extend the quarter section marks in on the top wood; otherwise they would be removed with the waste.

Band saw to outline and pencil in the long and short cross center lines with a straight edge. The same oval inlay routine should be followed as described in Chapter 1. The oval inlay shown for Table A is a design measuring 6″ x 9″ but a different size and pattern is a matter of choice. As described, saw close to the string outline of the design. Use hand tools to remove all background veneer. Turn paper side up, mark a long center line in pencil, also the cross center line, place oval on top, matching oval center lines to the corresponding lines on the top. Hold down without shifting, scribe a line around the circumference, deepen the outline with hand tools, rout out close to the line (photo 5-15). Trim the remainder with hand tools. Carefully enlarge the recess in spots for a perfect inlay fit.

Prepare a waste piece of ¾″ plywood slightly larger than the inlay and set four deep-throated clamps to reach in from the top edge (photo 5-16). With a roll of 1″ masking tape handy for use, everything will be ready for gluing. Coat the recess with glue, place perfectly in position, apply a strip of tape in length and one across (photo 5-17). Cover the tape with a sheet of paper, place the oval plywood exactly on top and clamp as shown in photo 5-16. Rough sand the oval to remove the paper and also to assure yourself that a good glue job was done.

Set the 1-16″ router bit to the depth of string inlay. Adjust the fence for a border cut of about ¾″ and groove the circumference (photo 5-18). Glue the inlay and seat in the groove. After setting, round the edge of top with a spoke shave, rough and fine sand the edge, then rough and fine sand the top surface, turn the top over and fine sand the underside.

Make two battens 13-16″ x 1″ x 15″ long, cut an ogee curve on all ends (see line drawing). Now measure for the ⅝″ dowel receiving holes. Put a temporary mark at the center of battens which will also be the center of the 3½″ block, now halve that and mark 1⅞″, now back up one half of the dowel diameter, or 5-16″; this comes to a final mark for the center of dowel hole 1 9-16″ past center of battens. Bore these holes as a pair and stop boring at a depth of 9-16″. Screw holes to fasten battens 1″ in from each end and one in the center. Sand all batten surfaces except the bottoms.

Turn the top upside down, stand the base also upside down on the top, fit the battens on dowels in working position, measure and shift the unit so the hinge block will be centered. Sink screws on a length to allow about ¼″ purchase in the top wood. The table catch will be attached after finishing materials have been applied (see finishing instructions in Chapter 15).

There are not many differences between tables A and B. Of course the post is

PHOTO 5-15

PHOTO 5-16

PHOTO 5-17

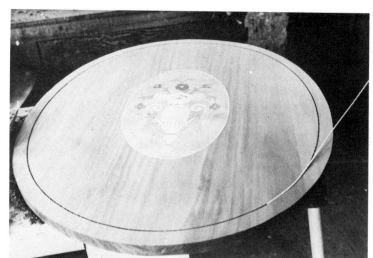

PHOTO 5-18

PHOTO 5-19

PHOTO 5-20

PHOTO 5–21

PHOTO 5–22

turned differently and many sizes must be checked with the line drawings. Notable differences are the 13-16″ thick leg wood. When tapering leg sides, set jointer depth to leave ½″ thick wood at the ankle. Instead of a curved fillet where ankle joins spade foot, there is a square shoulder.

If two tables are being made, observe the procedure in photos 5-17, 5-19, and 5-20. When gluing the ovals, only one piece waste plywood sawn to slightly larger than the inlay is needed. After covering the tape with paper, place the plywood accurately over one inlay and tape to hold (photo 5-19 on the left). Turn the other top upside down, place exactly on top of the first and tighten with four clamps as shown in photo 5-20.

6

Window Seat

MATERIALS

    4 leg blanks 1¾″ x 1¾″ x 28″ long
    4 scroll leg extensions 1⅛″ thick x 4″ wide x 9″ long
    2 arm turnings 1½″ x 1½″ x 15¾″
    2 arm panels 13-16″ x 5″ x 14¾″
    2 long seat rails 13-16″ x 3½″ x 30¼″
    2 short seat rails 13-16″ x 3½″ x 15¼″
    1 plywood seat board ⅜″ x 16¼″ x ½″

INLAY

    ovals 3½″ x 6½″ (2)
    ovals 1¼″ x 3″ (4)
    lengths ¼″ banding (3)
    length ½″ banding (1)
    lengths 1-16″ string (4)

THIS WINDOW SEAT IS, to me, reminiscent of the era of gracious living as depicted notably by Wallace Nutting in his sketches and watercolors. It does add variety to the normally commonplace seating equipment we live with today.

Start by making a stiff cardboard pattern of the full leg (detail blow-up). Before working on the legs, bring to completion the four seat rails made of 13-16″ thick wood—two long rails 3½″ x 30¼″ and two 3½″ x 15¼″. These are finished square-cut lengths and include ¾″ long tenons which will be made next. Set up

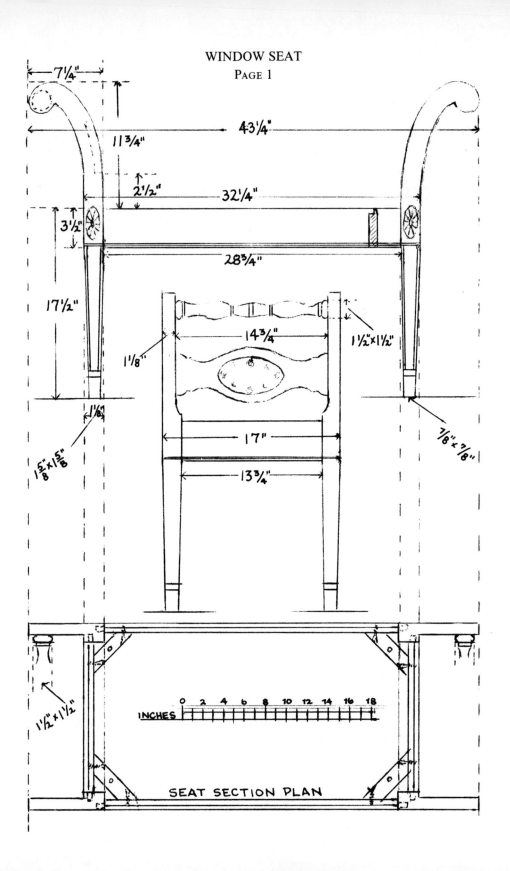

SEAT SECTION PLAN

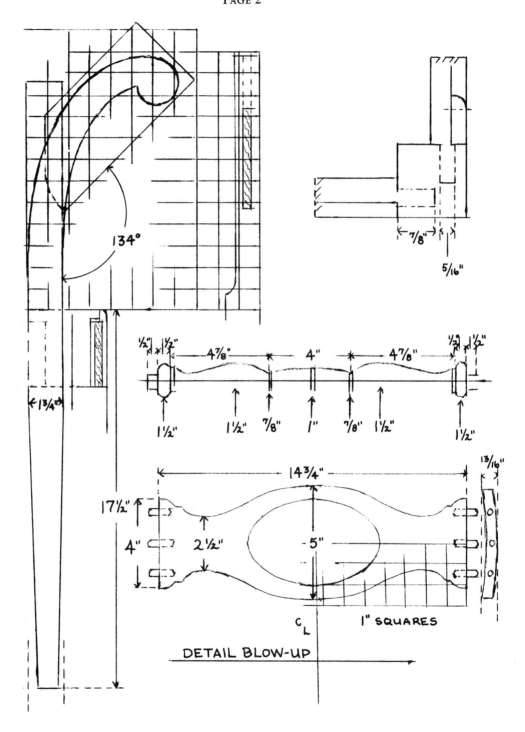

134°

7/8"

5/16"

½" x ½"   4⅞"   4"   4⅞"   ½" x ½"

1½"   1½"   7/8"   1"   7/8"   1½"   1½"

1¾"

14¾"

13/16"

17½"

4"   2½"   5"

C L

1" SQUARES

DETAIL BLOW-UP

the dado side cutters with a 5-16″ spacer washer between, raise to cut a depth of ¾″, set fence to allow a 5-16″ shoulder on the marked outside surface, pass all rail ends over this set-up. Use a combination saw blade to cut the inside and outside shoulders on these rail ends. Set the saw fence to cut ¾″ to the outside of the saw, measure the saw depth of cut to 5-16″ for the outside shoulder and 3-16″ for the inside.

Tenons will extend to the rail bottom edge but on the top (detail blow-up) they must be cut ½″ down so as not to interfere with a ⅜″ x ⅜″ rabbet provided for the upholstered seat board. Rabbet the four rails, round the top outside corner according to the line drawing. Mount the two dado side cutters for a ¼″ banding inlay groove which should start ⅛″ up from rail bottom; run these grooves to a depth equal to inlay thickness (photo 6-1).

Prepare four leg blanks 1¾″ x 1¾″ x 28″ long, group them together and mark the two right-angle sides of each for rail mortises (drawing of seat section plan). Pencil mark up from the bottom, 14″ and 17″, which is the tenon height and places the rails 17½″ above the floor. Chuck the 5-16″ machine bit in the drill press, adjust the fence to leave a 5-16″ space between, bore a line of holes between leg marks 13-16″ deep, straighten mortise walls with wide chisel, clean out with a narrow one, and repeat (photo 6-2).

Tapering the legs is done as described in Chapter 4. Determine how much wood is to be taken off of each side. In this case, it's a 1¾″ leg tapered to ⅞″, or a difference of ⅞″ which, divided in half, leaves 7-16″ to be removed from each side. That depth of cut is too much for one pass over the jointer, so make two cuts on each side as was done on the Sewing Table.

A quick repeat of instruction highlights: Mark jointer bed where knives will start to cut, lower leg to start cutting 1″ below bottom rail line for first cut, 2″ below for second cut. There will be a slight depression showing where each jointer cut started. Take a lightly set hand plane to even out these surfaces.

Set up the ½″ dado for ankle bands that start 2½″ up (photo 6-3). Group the legs in a four square and mark what will be the long sides as opposed to the ends. These leg positions must be kept in mind because the side surfaces will now be channeled for more inlay. Set up the router for a 1-16″ string cut with the fence setting for about ⅛″ in from the corner (photo 6-1). Run these grooves from the ankle bands up to the ¼″ rail band area so that the string ends will be cut to

PHOTO 6–1

PHOTO 6–2

PHOTO 6–3

length when the band line is extended across the leg with hand tools. Glue and place these string lines. After setting, rough sand.

The fan oval procedure follows Chapters 1 and 3 with photos 1-8, 1-9, 1-10, 1-12, and 1-13 applicable in this case. After removing background veneer to the oval outline, position the inlay about ¼″ above what will be the rail band line. As instructed, hold firmly, scribe a line around the oval, deepen the line with #3 and #4 gouges, rout out close to this line, remove remaining wood with hand tools. After final fitting, glue the receiving depressions, position ovals with paper side up, tape to hold in place, cover each oval with paper, place one leg on top of the other with inlay face to face, line them up exactly and clamp (photo 6-3). Repeat with the other pair of legs.

The reason for adding wing extensions to the legs instead of using one board is to give more strength in the area of the scroll. See blow-up drawing where the extending piece 1⅛″ thick by 4″ wide by 9″ long is superimposed on 1″ squares. One end of these extensions is angled to 134°.

Mount the dado side cutters on saw mandrel using a ⅜″ spacer between. Set fence to cut ⅜″ x ⅞″ long tongues in the center of wood thickness. That breaks down to ⅜″ tongue and two ⅜″ shoulders (photo 6-4). Next, cut away the waste shoulder wood (photo 6-5) and remove a rough radius on the long point of each piece to correspond to the receiving groove planned for the legs. This waste cut can be observed on the blow-up.

Since 1⅛″ thick wood is all we want up in the arm area, that portion of the leg will be brought down to that thickness. "Now listen good," as a testy instructor would say. "If you don't want to make one or two new legs, you'd better pick the right surface on each leg to run the groove." Good advice. A safe action to follow now would be to group the legs in their proper position, checking to see that mortises are placed right; then mark the top end of each piece where the ⅜″ groove is to be cut. A groove surface is superimposed on the 1″ square blow-up which also shows where and how far down the leg wood will be cut away to leave 1⅛″ thickness. This leg wood is to be removed directly opposite the oval inlay (photo 6-6).

Slide a wing extension in place. Without glue, lay the pattern on top, check to see that a full pattern outline can be made without running off of the wood at any point. Measure the distance down from the leg top to the junction and mark.

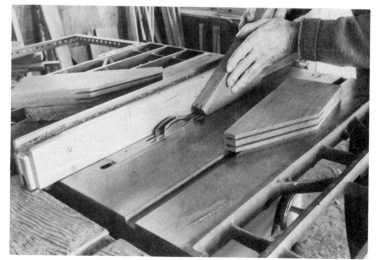

PHOTO 6-4

PHOTO 6-5

PHOTO 6-6

That will show where to place the remaining three. Glue both grooves and tongues, seat tightly, set overnight. Place pattern on each and outline (photo 6-7). Bandsaw to lines, rough sand all surfaces down to inlay (photo 6-8).

Use the small handmade miter box to cut 16 pieces of ½″ banding inlay 1″ long for ankles; glue in as instructed in Chapter 4. After setting, rough sand all lower leg surfaces.

Assemble an end unit without glue, use a bar clamp to draw tight, measure accurately the distance between upper legs. The drawing calls for 14¾″ but, if there should be any variation from drawing, use the actual measurement. Cut two pieces of 13-16″ wood 5″ x 14¾″ for the decorative panels. The easiest way to end up with four identical curved sections is to start with a piece of cardboard 5″ x 14¾″, lay off one quarter into 1″ squares as shown on drawing blow-up, and draw in the curved outline. Now carefully cut to this line, using a fine tooth jigsaw blade. Use the waste piece to turn over and mark the other end. This will give you a half pattern as shown in photo 6-9 which is all that is needed, but if a full pattern is desired, finish the other side.

Place pattern and outline both wood panels, bandsaw, rough and fine sand edges but not ends. Lay a leg flat, upend a panel and position 2½″ up from the rail top edge, pencil mark the leg curve on to panel end. This is just a rough guide line to remove most of the wood from the face or crowned side. Plane as shown in photo 6-10. Turn the panel over, hold in vise and roughly concave the back surface for a uniform thickness curved panel. Repeat with number two. Rough and fine sand.

I have found occasional need for a plane to dish out concave surfaces. At the time I did not know whether or not one could be purchased so I remodeled a wooden flat bed, slightly curved the bed and ground the blade to match (photo 6-11).

Panels will be joined to the legs with three 5-16″ dowels in each end. No dowel measuring is necessary if this method is followed: pencil spot where you want to bore for dowels in each end, tap a ¾″ brad in each spot to a depth of about ¼″, use wire cutters to cut brads about 3-32″ above wood surface. The accuracy of the 2½″ mark made above the rail line is not nearly as important as the need for marking the three other legs exactly the same. This must be done to keep the whole end unit square when it is finally assembled.

PHOTO 6-7

PHOTO 6-8

PHOTO 6-9

Photo 6-10

Photo 6-11

Photo 6-12

Upend a panel and carefully place the bottom edge on the 2½″ mark, keeping the face close to the leg line but not below it, so that more wood can be removed from the panel but not from the leg curve. When panel is accurately placed, press with sufficient pressure to mark the leg with the cut brads (mark leg area and panel end with an identifying 1, 2, 3, 4). Repeat with the other three panel ends. Pull the cut brads from panel wood, make a larger and better mark in each with an awl. Also enlarge the leg marks.

Legs can be bored on the drill press using a 5-16″ machine bit. Bore to a depth of slightly more than ¾″ for a 5-16″ x 1½″ spiral dowel. Boring the panel ends must be done with a brace and bit or a hand power drill. If a drill is used, a starting hole about 3-16″ deep must be made with the brace and bit to keep the drill from creeping.

Two arm turnings should be made next. To determine the length of blanks, start with the exact length of curved panel just worked on. Add to that ½″ on each end for a ¾″ diameter dowel and an extra inch on each end to be removed after turning. When turning, as suggested in Chapter 5, be prepared with a few extra blanks in case of spoilage. Blanks are 1½″ x 1½″ (photo 6-12).

On the end rail surface of each leg, center mark the scroll for a ¾″ dowel hole about 9-16″ deep. Use the drill press to assure a true right-angle hole. Photo 6-13 shows all the parts for one end which, after rough sanding can now be glued together permanently (photo 6-14).

Photo 6-15 shows the front surface of a panel being hand planed flush with the leg curvature. Be sure to end up with a true uniform radius having no dips because the surface must have a thin inlay oval inserted. Rough sand.

Prepare the two oval inlays 3½″ x 6½″ or some other choice, by following oval preparation routine described in previous chapters. There is an important difference between these inserts and others; in this case they are imbedded in a curved surface whereas in most others the surface is flat. Marking (photo 6-16), routing, and fitting follow the usual procedures. Before gluing, have ready to use a piece of ¼″ plywood larger than the oval. This must be ¼″ thick to allow bending under clamp pressure. Have four C clamps, 1″ masking tape, and a sheet of paper handy. Glue the recess, fit oval in place (paper side up), try to hold the inlay down as close as possible with three strips of tape, cover with paper, and place the plywood on top of that. Place clamps over the long ends and the shorter

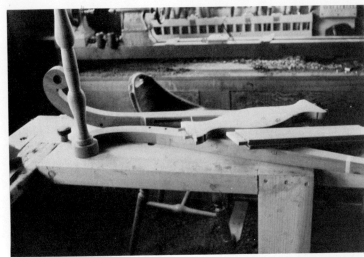

PHOTO 6–13

PHOTO 6–14

PHOTO 6–15

sides, draw tight, set overnight (photo 6-17). Hand sand these ovals with coarse paper over a block to remove the paper backing; then do the usual rough and fine sanding over the whole panel. Repeat with the second one.

Check to be sure that the leg and end rail junctures are flush; if not, sand or plane to make both pieces even because the inlay channel must be carried over the leg.

Before gluing the long rails in place, it will be more convenient to finish channeling and placing the ¼″ band inlay along the bottom edge of end rails. Hold a thin straight edge *in the groove,* butting along one side and extending out over the leg to be marked. Scratch a line with a needlepoint scriber across the leg. Place a straight edge against the other wall of the groove, scratch that line. Now you have two straight accurate lines to follow with the extra fine tooth saw (photo 6-1). Saw to about the inlay depth; use a 3-16″ wide chisel to clean out the channel. Do this on the legs of both end units. Glue in the banding inlay, allowing a little to extend over the leg edge, set overnight, remove the protruding inlay.

Coat the long rail mortises and tenons with glue, enter tenons in mortises, span each rail with bar clamp, tighten and check with a large square. If minor adjustment is needed, shift one clamp to have a pad cover only half of the leg surface. Do this on the opposite corner with the other clamp. If you chose the right pad to shift, the necessary correction should have been made; if not, work the pad on the other end.

Follow immediately with corner blocks made of secondary wood (photo 6-18). An ideal size for these is 1¾″ x 1¾″ in a long length. Hold this piece under the rails, across a corner, rough out a right-angle notch where the leg will be, hold again under the rails and pencil mark along each rail, carefully band saw to these lines, and check for fit. Repeat with three more corners, marking each block and its respective corner. Bore through each block end with a 3-16″ drill, for 1½″ #8 flat head wood screws. Position these holes where the wood will be about ¾″ thick allowing ½″ of screw to be turned into the rail. After boring, glue block surfaces making contact with the rails, hold block about ⅛″ below rabbets, sink screws. Look again at photo 6-18.

After glue setting, check the long rail and leg joints, if they are not flush, sand or plane where necessary. Repeat the scratch line procedure followed on the end units to extend the banding grooves (photo 6-1). Glue and seat the banding,

Photo 6-16

Photo 6-17

PHOTO 6-18

PHOTO 6-19

PHOTO 6-20

letting it extend slightly over the corners, set overnight. Rough sand this newly laid inlay and go over the whole bench with #120 grit paper, examining the piece carefully for any missed surfaces and sharp corners which must be blunted with sandpaper. For instructions on applying finishing materials see Chapter 15.

Make two ⅜″ plywood boards for upholstery that will measure (when butted together) the rabbeted opening less ⅛″ all around. The butted sides must be beveled toward the bottom so that when raised in the center (photo 6-19) for insertion, the butted edges will not spread apart. Two battens fastened with screws will hold the halves as a single unit for upholstering (photo 6-20).

The drawing plan shows how the upholstered board must be notched out at each corner to fit around the legs. These cut-outs should be made to leave ⅛″ space. Also shown on the plan are screw holes bored down through the corner blocks to hold the upholstered board when inserted and ready for use.

If you have had no upholstering experience and wish to try, this board does not require any particular expertise. You will need a piece of foam rubber 1″ thick the overall size of the board and a piece of unbleached muslin 6 or 8 inches larger each way than the board and stretched over the foam, tacked about every inch on the ⅜″ thick edge. This can be done evenly if tacking is started about the center on each side, seating three or four #3 tacks on one side, then stretched on the opposite side and tacked with about eight tacks, returning to the first side to continue tacking further first on one side then the other. Do the board ends in like manner. Cut off the waste muslin with scissors. Your covering material will be stretched and tacked on the board bottom about 2″ in from the edge instead of tacking on the ⅜″ edge (photo 6-20). To give it a professional look, black cambric must be tacked on the board bottom *but* not before the battens have been removed and the center raised to permit insertion in the frame (photo 6-19). After the board is placed, turn the whole piece over and rest the board on a flat surface to refasten the battens, then tack down the black cambric which will cover the entire bottom, battens and all. Finally four 2½″ #8 screws through the blocks will complete your creation.

If you aren't certain you'll do a good job, and would rather have an upholsterer do the board, show him this book so he'll know how it must be inserted.

7

Martha Washington Chair Frame

MATERIALS

 1 plank 2″ x 9″ x 8 ft. long (This will probably take care of all parts
  but maple rails and cross pieces.)
 1 piece hard or soft maple 1″ x 8″ x 8 ft. long
  (Have this piece skin
  surfaced, which means that all saw marks
  probably will not be removed but maximum
  thickness is retained.)
 spiral dowels 5-16″ x 1½″ and ⅜″ x 1½″

INLAY

 18″ of ½″ banding
 4 lengths 1-16″ string inlay

MARTHA WASHINGTON or Lolling chairs can truthfully be called "timeless" in design. Detail and motif variations are infinite but basic size and proportions are always much the same. I truly believe you will achieve great satisfaction in building this frame.

Where the back leg piece continues above the seat to become part of the back, it is called a style and will distinguish the back from the front legs.

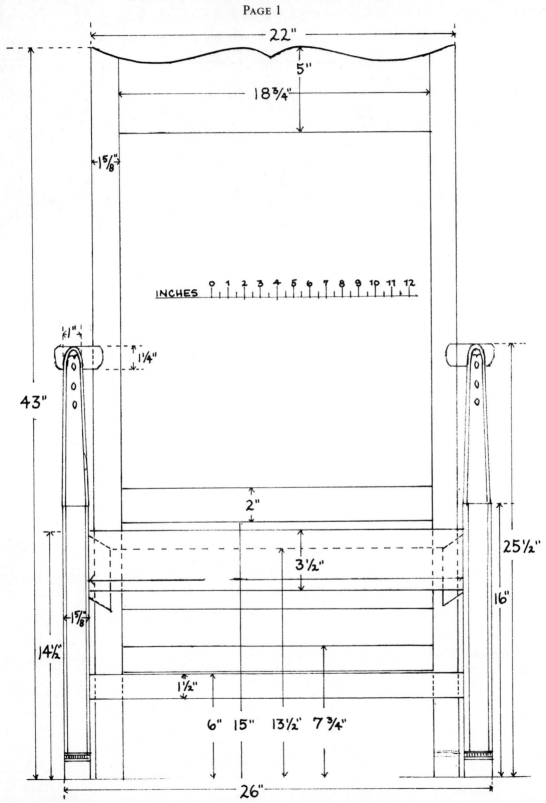

MARTHA WASHINGTON CHAIR FRAME
PAGE 2

6 5/8" POINT
INCHES
0 1 2 3 4 5 6 7 8 9 10 11 12 13 14
1" SQUARES
25"
43"
7 5/8"
3"
6"
17 1/2"
21 3/4"
87°
1 5/8"
1 5/8"
16"

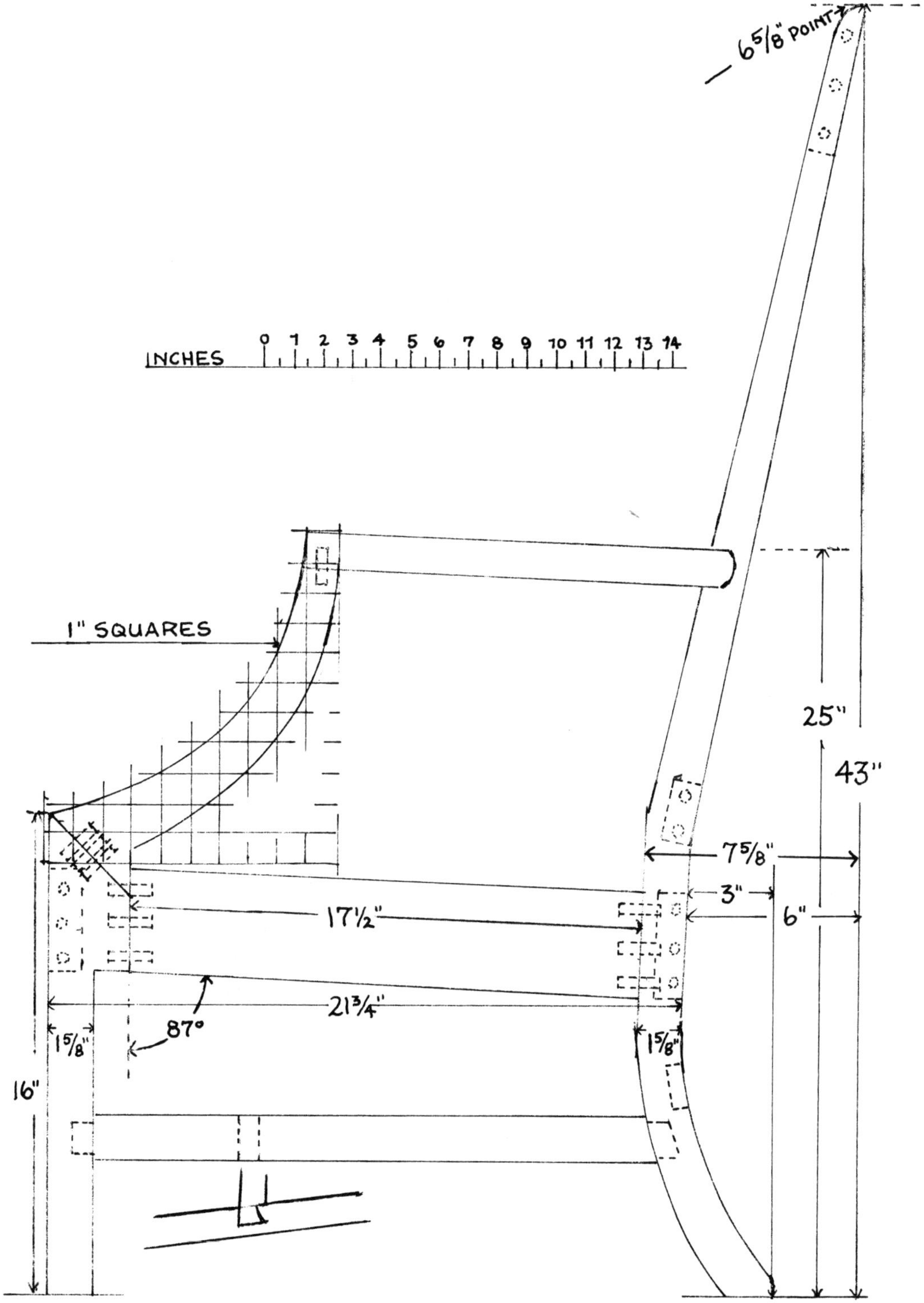

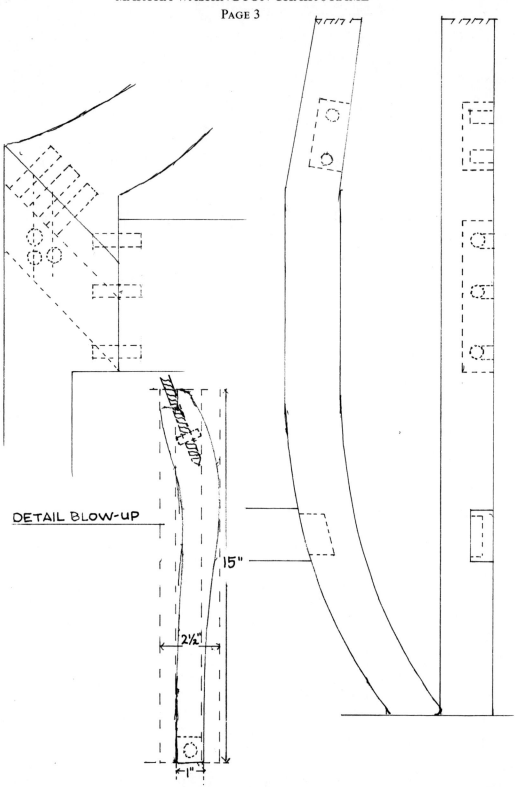

DETAIL BLOW-UP

15"

2½"

1"

Cardboard or other stiff material can be used for a pattern which must be 43″ long by at least 7⅝″ wide, (see drawing). Along one straight edge, mark where the side and back rails will join the styles, bottom mark 10″, top 13½″. Continue the straight edge line another 2½″ above the rail mark before sloping to the 43″ point measured from front to back 6⅝″ with the back point the full 7⅝″ width.

Below the rail line, continue 1″ straight before starting the curve which should swing in on the pattern board about 3½″ to complete the inside line. Now measure and mark at about 2″ intervals, the outside line 1⅝″ wide up to the 2½″ mark above rail. From that point to the top, the wood width tapers, on a straight line, to one inch. If the style wood is thicker than 1⅝″, it may be reduced to that measurement on the circular saw after band sawing to pattern outline.

A pattern must be made for the front leg and arm and arm support unit. Measure up the straight edge of pattern board 16″, which is the point where the leg wood is mitered for the support. Finish the leg outline with a parallel line 1⅝″ from the front to a height of 10″. There a right-angle shoulder extends back 1⅜″ to another parallel line making the wood 3″ wide. This 3″ line will reach up from the 10″ shoulder point where the back or under side of the support starts its curve. Lay off the pattern board into 1″ squares (line drawing), pencil in the front and back curves, remembering to accurately square off the top for arm attachment.

Leg and support wood is 1⅝″ thick and they are joined together before pattern is laid and outlined (photo 7-1). Each piece is oversized until sawed to outline. Observe drawing blow-up to see that three joining ⅜″ x 1½″ dowels are clustered together because the area of joining surfaces will not permit placing them in line.

Miter to 45° the top end of leg pieces. Supports must have the grain run in as straight a line as possible with the general direction of the curved shape. To find this angle, lay a support piece flat, lay a leg on top at one end, and place the pattern to get an approximate line of direction; a temporary pencil line along the leg miter will show the miter degree needed on the support pieces.

Determine the close area where dowels can be placed, tap in three ¾″ brads (about halfway) leaving not less than ¼″ walls between dowels. Cut the brads with wire cutters about 3-32″ above wood surface, lay this piece on a flat surface, slide the support up to it and position so that the pattern, when placed, will cover the wood completely. Press the two together to mark the support for dowel boring. Pull the cut nails, deepen the nail marks with an awl, use brace and bit to start all ⅜″ holes, finish boring with the portable drill to slightly more than ¾″.

Twirl a small diameter dowel stick covered with glue in each leg hole, tap in dowels, coat support holes and press together, using a rubber mallet if necessary to seat tightly. Repeat (photo 7-1), set overnight. Place pattern, outline and band saw.

Tapering the curved arm supports is a repeat performance of leg tapers from 1⅝″ down to one inch, half of ⅝″ and half again, making two passes on the jointer. Lower leg unit to start the cut about where the underside curve starts.

Now will be a good time to work on all the maple parts. Maple is recommended because it resists splintering and is hard enough to hold upholstery tacks tightly. The chair back is the same width from top to bottom so all cross members will be the same length. Cut one top piece from the 15-16″ maple board 5″ wide x 18¾″ long. A 2″ x 18¾″ piece is needed for the upholsterer to end the back material. A back seat rail, sized to 3½″ x 18¾″, plus a primary wood stretcher 1½″ x ½″ x 18¾″, plus 1½″ for tenons (the maple parts are joined to styles with dowels; no need for extra wood in length). When sawing the back seat rail to width the side and front rails can be cut on the same set-up, leaving them in the rough length.

Cut the 1½″ x ½″ stretcher 20¼″ long, set up the dado with a ¼″ spacer, raised to cut ¾″ in height. Set fence to place tenons fully on one side surface leaving a ¼″ shoulder on the other. Replace dado with fine tooth saw to remove the shoulder waste wood.

Check for placement of back cross members on line drawing, marking the style where the top edge of each will be doweled in. Set a scratch gauge to mark cross piece ends about center in thickness, mark the outside and top edges with X's so measuring for dowels will be done from the right point on rails and styles. Use the same gauge setting to scratch lines on styles to match the cross pieces, make all dowel boring measurements from cross piece top edges. Line drawing and blow-up show number of dowels and their relative position from top to bottom. When measuring down for dowel boring points, accurately place a fine pencil line across the scratch mark. Repeat on the styles and mark the junction points with an awl. Bore all ⅜″ holes 13-16″ deep, starting them with a brace and bit. A machine bit in the drill press will assure aligned holes in the styles and front legs. Use a portable drill for the maple pieces.

Using a combination saw, square the ends of the front rail to 22¾″. Observe the line drawing side view. The side rail drops 1″ in height from front to back, which translates into about 3° and the chair front, 4″ wider than the back, necessitates another angle of about 3° off 90°. The back end of side rails will be cross cut square but the saw will be angled to 3° for the same cut. Remember these rails will be a right and left when the front ends are cut on a compound angle. A good suggestion to follow: after back end cutting, edge up the side rails in the right and left position, mark TOP on the visible edge of each and draw an exaggerated angled line to show which way the 3° cut is to be made. You will realize when working this compound angle out in your mind that the cross cut gauge must be set 3° to one side of 90° for one rail and 3° to the other side for the second rail.

Scratch mark all three rails and their receiving areas on styles and front legs. Mark for dowels measuring down from the top. Press an awl in each junction for a bit starting mark. Brace and bit for a starting hole to be followed with a portable drill slightly angled by eyesight. Front rail ends are bored at right-angle.

Twirl a glue-coated small dowel stick to insert into all rail and cross member dowel holes, seat each dowel, using a small hammer. Photo 7-2 shows all chair parts worked up to this point.

Coat all cross member style holes plus the small back stretcher mortise with glue, press all cross pieces into their respective places by hand, coat the other style holes, enter cross pieces, use three bar clamps to draw the unit tight.

Now the front leg units must be inlaid and finished up to the point of joining other parts for a complete chair unit. The ½″ ankle band groove should be routed 1″ above the bottom. As with other ankle bands, this is usually done on the saw table with a dado set-up. But in this case all four leg surfaces will not lie flat on the table so the portable router must be used. Set the fence for a 1″ starting cut, bit depth equal to banding thickness. Set the 1-16″ router bit to 1-28″ depth and the fence for ⅛″ in from the corner. Groove for string inlay up the front leg surfaces, starting in the band grooves and continuing to the top or start of the curve (photo 7-3).

Photo 7-1

Photo 7-2

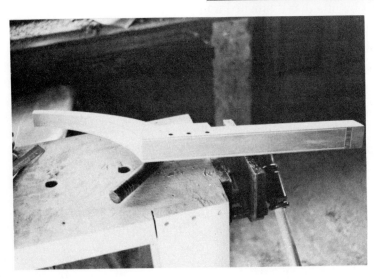

Photo 7-3

Because of the concave curve, the string groove must be cut in with a specially altered scratch gauge. Purchase the least expensive scratch gauge, file the hardened point, tapering it both forward and backward so it can be used effectively either way depending on grain direction. In width, carefully file the steel to cut 1-16″ leaving straight walls on both sides. These last filings are, of course, at right-angle to the gauge bar.

Set the gauge to cut matching grooves as a continuation of those coming up the front (photo 7-4). If you have filed the tapers to leave a sharp cutting edge, a few strokes of the gauge, going with the wood grain, will leave a satisfactory groove. Reverse stroke direction when entering area against the grain. Do not glue in string inlay on the curves at this time.

If the dowels are not already glued in the front and side seat rails do it at this time but do not coat the receiving holes in front legs and styles with glue. Assemble the frame, drawing it up tight with bar clamps. Measure and mark 6″ up on the front legs and styles (line drawing). These marks represent the top edge of side stretchers. The marks on styles should not follow the style curvature but be a perpendicular measurement. Check the rough length of side and center stretchers, preparing three pieces ½″ thick by 1½″ high. The front ends of the side stretchers are to be cross cut at 90°. Tenons on these ends can be made on the dado with a ¼″ space between, angle the mandrel about 3°, raise cutters to ¾″ height. Set fence to cut the ¼″ tenons all on one side leaving a ¼″ shoulder so sufficient leg wood remains on the outside corner after the matching mortise is prepared.

Up to this point, there is no right or left because either ½″ edge can be used for the top. Now hold a stretcher even with both 6″ high marks making sure the slight angle is bearing in the right direction. Using a pencil, draw a line on stretcher wood to follow the style curvature. Set a bevel gauge to this line which will be used to mark for both side stretchers. Measure exactly the distance from corner of leg to style corner at the 6″ marks. Measure the same distance on the stretcher starting at the front shoulder. The mark just made will be the back shoulder and the point where the pre-set bevel will mark a line on stretcher wood from top to bottom on the outside surface. Mark another beveled line ¾″ past the first one; this will be the end of the tenon and can be cut with a hand saw.

There are only two more tenons to make and they could be done by hand unless the dado set-up is still available and the saw table fence can be used on the left side of saw blade. These stretchers now are definitely right and left. Caution: a little inattention when cutting these back tenons will give you a good reason to make another pair. Place the stretchers on the saw table, front ends away from you with the shoulders on the outside surfaces. On the near or back ends, mark for shoulders plus exaggerated lines showing which way the 3° angles will bear on each. One tenon, it will be found, must be cut with the fence on the right and the other on the left. Top and bottom shoulders on all ends can be done with a hand saw.

When laying off for mortises, check the width of shoulders plus half or ⅛″ of the tenon; that will be the boring center line. The frame can now be disassembled and mortises cut and fitted. Rough and fine sand the inside and back surfaces of the front leg units plus inside and front style surfaces up to the rails. Stretchers should be sanded on top and on inside surfaces. Glue-coat the remaining dowel holes, hand press all parts together, circle the frame with a heavy strap clamp or four bar clamps to draw tight, check for square. Set overnight.

Turn upside down on the work table and from the front legs mark the side stretchers 5″ back. Edge up the center stretcher, place at the marks, and pencil line the bottom edge along the side stretchers (photo 7-5). Make another parallel line 5-16″ farther out for the length of the dovetail on each end. Take a long look at photo 7-6. It shows that because of the wider front, the front surface already has enough flair so all of the shoulder waste wood will be removed from the back. Cut down along the side stretcher line 5-16″ and remove that much wood from the dovetail top. Now edge up the stretcher and equalize any variation there might be from the side stretcher marks. Draw the piece backward to where it will fit tight; then, as shown on 7-6, scribe the dovetail outline.

Using a square, scratch a continuation of the two outlines down the inside surface. The receiving socket will end 5-16″ below stretcher top surface. This is known as a blind dovetail. Start a ¼″ hole inside the dovetail lines with a brace and bit, put a bit stop on the portable drill to stop boring at 1 3-16″. Carefully line up the drill both ways and bore both holes. Use the finest tooth back saw available to saw on the inside surface lines on the bottom surface. Be careful that the saw does not cut into the top surface. Use an exceptionally sharp ¼″ chisel to shave the dovetail walls for a close fit (photo 7-7).

Photo 7-4

Photo 7-5

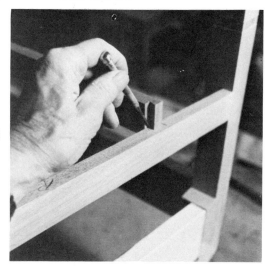

Photo 7-6

The arms are made of 1⅛″ thick wood 2½″ wide by 17″ long. This is 2″ longer than the drawing shows but it is safer to cut to length after the back end has been notched and fitted to the style. Since there are two alike, it may be well to make a cardboard pattern using the drawing blow-up as a guide. Leave the extra wood length on the front end where the width is an even 1″. Notch out the pattern about ¾″ each way on one corner. Band saw the wood to this pattern outline. Mark the style 25″ from floor to proposed top of arm, hold wood arm piece flat on support top surface which should bring the back end close to the style mark. If there is any variation, it is more important to seat the front perfectly than to try meeting the back line. The notch will have to be angled to match the front slope of the style and possibly a slight adjustment made on the side.

When fitted in the rear, place the arm in its permanent position, holding the front on center over the support, pencil line around the support, repeat on the second arm. Now put a marking nail in the center of support top surface, cut it to 3-32″, replace arm, hold over support, matching the penciled line to the support outline, press to mark the nail end. Deepen the nail marks with an awl and start the ⅜″ holes with a brace and bit. Use the drill press for the dowel hole in the arm and portable drill for the support, both holes to be 13-16″ deep. Repeat with other arm. Glue the 1½″ spiral dowel in the support but not in the arm. Seat the arm tightly on the front dowel; if necessary, use a bar clamp for a tight fit. Bring the other arm up to this point, span the two arms, close to the back with a bar clamp to hold tightly in place for bolt boring.

Counterbore a ½″ hole into the style slightly below center of the arm wood. This is to provide a solid seat for the 3-16″ x 3½″ round head bolt to be used as the fastening agent (see line drawing blow-up). Bore through the style and into the arm for a total distance of more than 3½″ with a 7-32″ drill. It is most important that the drill is kept in line horizontally below arm center thickness. Lateral direction must also be watched carefully. Remove the cross clamp and the arms. It will probably be necessary to continue drilling the bolt holes to get the desired depth.

Grind a stubby point on the bolt to make it easier to enter the embedded nut. Slide the bolt through the style hole to measure how far into the arm it will extend, back off ½″ to drill for a square nut. Slide a straight stick into the hole for direction, draw a pencil line on arm bottom surface directly over the stick, measure the predetermined distance to where the nut will be sunk. Draw a line at right-angle and across the bolt line for a series of 5-32″ holes extending ¼″ each side of the bolt line. Bore to a depth of what you think will allow the nut to be in line with the bolt. This slot can be straight walled with a small chisel or, at the time of boring, lower the drill a little at a time and slide the arm along the slot to gradually deepen it. Clean out chips from slot and hole, drop nut in place, enter bolt in hole and engage the nut threads. Turn the bolt in to the end of the hole to pull the nut forward in the slot, pack the slot around and over the nut with plastic wood to keep it in place. The bolt can remain in place until final assembly.

Square cut the front ends of arms on the support line made when doweling. Use a spoke shave to finish shaping the arms but do not remove any wood on the last 3″ of the front ends. The arms have a more pleasing look if the outside curve toward the back is sloped inward on the bottom. The two bottom corners can be rounded slightly, the top outside corner should start at the back with a radius of about ⅜″, increasing as it comes forward. The inside corner starts at the back with a ¾″ radius which may increase slightly. Finish sand all surfaces up to the front ends. Remove bolts, glue-coat arm dowel holes, seat in place (be sure the notch is in place on the style), enter and start the bolt into the nut. If necessary, use a bar clamp for a tight joint on the arm support, finish drawing tight the long bolt. Repeat on other arm and set overnight.

Now a look at photo 7-8 will show how the arms are increasingly rounded as they approach the front end and, at the tip, the curve is even more than a half round; it could be called an arch. Look at the whole arm and if it looks clumsy at any point, carefully reshape for the desired improvement. Sand all these newly worked surfaces including the front cut which continues the support curve.

A piece of dogwood, holly, or any white veneer is needed to make the little decorations on the front arm supports. Pencil in a continuation of the string grooves that come up the supports, carry them around the top to determine the size and shape of the inlay. Cut two pieces to outline. Now six slim pointed ovals will be needed to complete the decorations. Place and scribe these inlays, marking each because of size variation. All recesses must be cut by hand using small chisels and #3 gouges. The short span of uncut string grooves could be done with

PHOTO 7-7

PHOTO 7-8

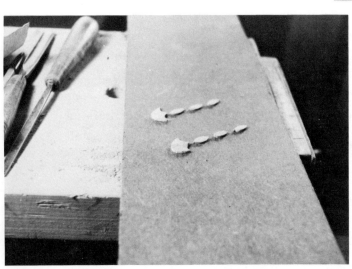

PHOTO 7-9

Photo 7-10

the scratch gauge if the setting is still the same (photos 7-8 and 7-9). Glue and seat the inlays, set overnight, then rough and fine sand the inlaid surfaces (photo 7-10).

No mention has been made of the fact that the crest rail on the back is to be rounded up to a high point at the back corner.

Carefully go over the whole chair, feeling for sharp corners especially where upholstery materials will cover. Remove any sharpness with a #60 sandpaper covered block. Consult Chapter 15 for finishing instructions.

If you are skilled in upholstery, even in an amateur way, that is fine. If not, have a professional do the job.

8

Pembroke Table

MATERIALS

4 legs 1⅝″ x 1⅝″ x 28″ long

top and leaves 12 sq. ft. ¾″ thick

side skirts and supports 13-16″ x 4½″ x 28″ long

drawer front and back skirt 2 pieces 2″ x 4½″ x 20″

drawer support and upper strip 2 pieces ⅝″ x 3″ x 20″

⅜″ thick poplar wood for drawer sides and bottom

INLAY

8 ovals 1⅜″ x 2⅞″

8 leg drops 6″ long in veneer background

18″ of ½″ banding

2 lengths ¼″ banding

3½″ lengths ⅛″ banding

10 lengths 1-16″ string inlay

HARDWARE

brass knob 1¼″ Dia. (1)

EVEN IN THESE MODERN TIMES many of us, if we would stop to think about it, still like a touch of gracious living which could not be better exemplified than in this Pembroke or breakfast table. Because the legs are inlaid all around, the table can be used anywhere, even in the center of a room.

So many operations in the construction of this table are repetitive that only the different ones will be dealt with thoroughly.

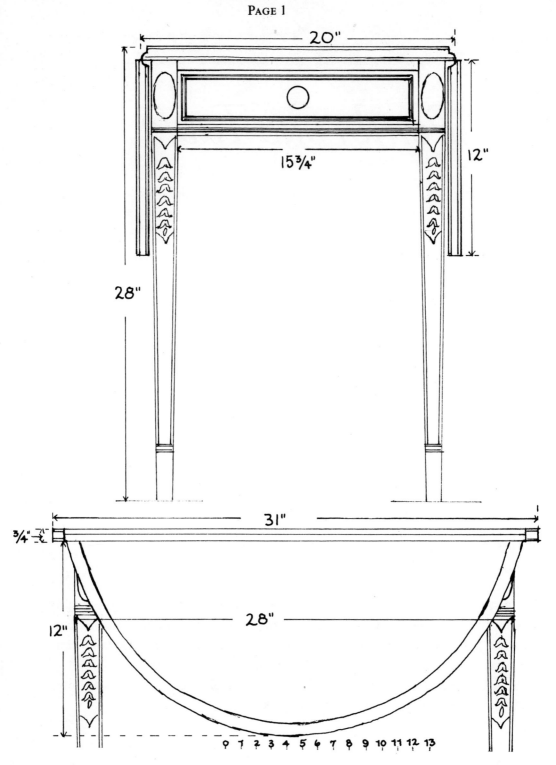

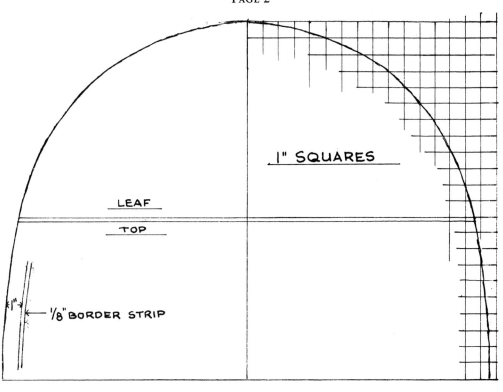

1" SQUARES

LEAF

TOP

1/8" BORDER STRIP

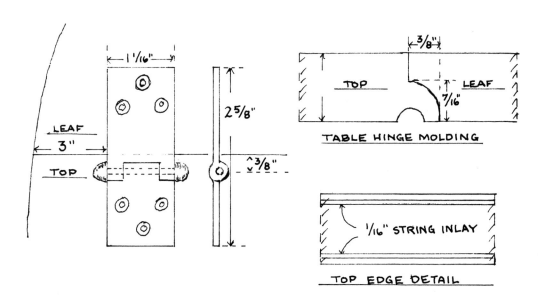

LEAF

TOP

1 1/16"

2 5/8"

3/8"

LEAF
3"

TOP

3/8"

TOP

3/8"

LEAF

7/16"

TABLE HINGE MOLDING

1/16" STRING INLAY

TOP EDGE DETAIL

DETAIL BLOW-UP

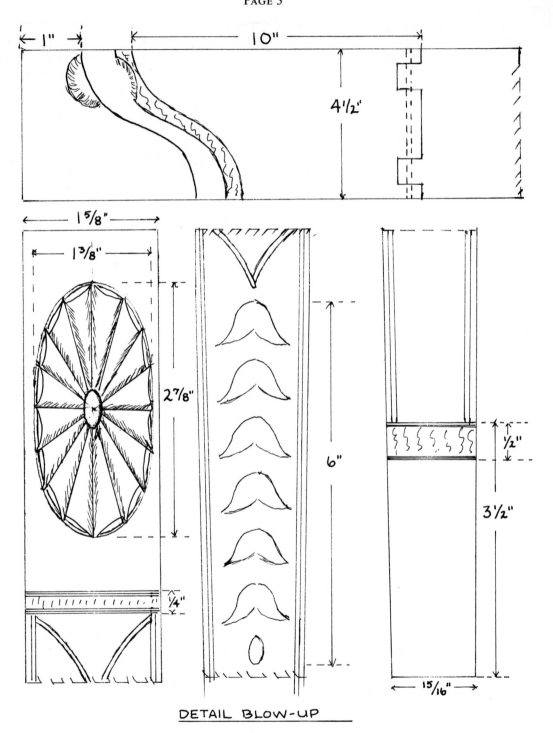

DETAIL BLOW-UP

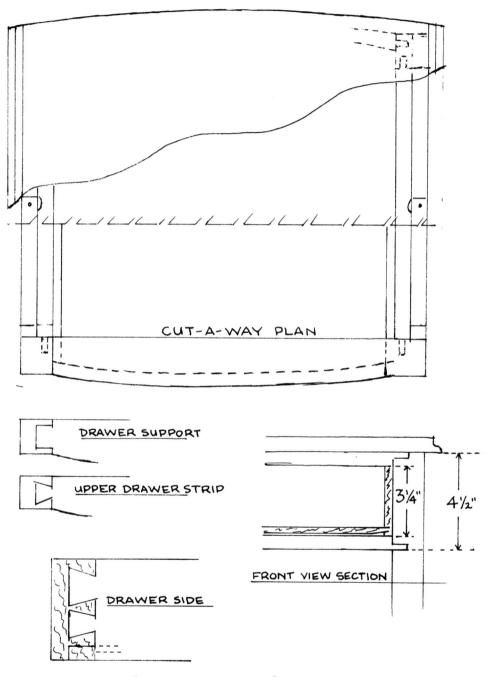

CUT-A-WAY PLAN

DRAWER SUPPORT

UPPER DRAWER STRID

DRAWER SIDE

FRONT VIEW SECTION

3¼"   4½"

DETAIL BLOW-UP

Saw four leg blanks 1⅝″ x 1⅝″ x 27¼″. Usually this is done first so two can be held together to determine the length of skirt pieces. Here we have twice 1⅝″ or 3¼″ and when working on the side skirts, the drawing calls for 28″ overall. So 28″ less 3¼″ = 24¾″ plus 1½″ for two ¾″ long tenons. All this translates into two pieces 13-16″ x 4½″ x 26¼″. Front and back pieces are measured in the same way: 20″ top, 19″ leg width overall, 15¾″ between legs, plus 1½″ tenons = 17¼″ long by (back piece) 2″ thick by 4½″ wide. The front calls for two strips ⅝″ thick by 3″ wide by 17¼″ long.

Set up the dado for 5-16″ tenons ¾″ long. Set the fence to leave a 5-16″ shoulder on one side of the side skirts and the same on the back. The back piece is 2″ thick which provides wood for the oval curvature. The two front strips should be done on the same dado set-up with possibly a minor adjustment to place the tenons fully on one flat surface line (drawing, front section). Remove all waste shoulder wood. Reduce the height of side and back tenons by cutting a ⅜″ shoulder on top and bottom edges. Shown on line drawing is the strip end treatment; the support has a traditional tenon while the upper strip is shaped into a dovetail.

Upend and group together the four leg blanks marking the tops "front" and "back," also roughly drawing in the tenon positions in each leg. Unless this is done with care, some mortises may be placed wrong. Follow instructions for the drawer support mortises in Chapter 4. It will also help if the instructions and photos for rail mortises in Chapter 6 are studied.

Leg tapering routine is fully explained in Chapters 4 and 6. The line drawing blow-up on page 3 for this table shows the legs tapered to 15-16″ at the bottom and shows the ½″ ankle band as being 3″ up. (See also photo 8-1.)

If a pattern is made now for one quarter of the top oval, it may also be used for the front supports and back skirt. The line drawing shows a quarter section laid off in one inch squares. If the squares are drawn on the pattern board, following the outline should not be too difficult. After it is ready, use the applicable section to draw off the necessary curve on supports and the back skirt.

Look at the drawing blow-up marked drawer support which shows the strip having tenon shoulders cut to place the back edge flush with the inside leg surface. The front shoulder will, of course, be cut to the front edge of the 3″ piece. The curve will start at the front leg corner. Use the same procedure for the upper strip but instead of a straight tenon, draw the dovetail shape. Remove saw marks from drawer support with a spoke shave, rough sand and rout out a ¼" groove ⅛" up from the bottom corner. This is done now so the piece can be inserted in the mortise for an accurate measurement to continue the banding line across the legs. The router groove can also be done ⅛" up on the back skirt. Check to be sure the front and back grooves are the same distance down from the top of legs.

Because of the flat surfaces, it is best to use the ¼" dado. Set the fence to match (from the top down) the banding line on support and skirt. Mark two right-angle sides on each leg. Be sure you have the right surfaces marked on each. Hold each leg against the cross cut gauge when making a pass over the dado (photo 8-2). Use the 1-16" cutter in the router for string inlay that reaches from the ¼" top band to the ½" ankle band ⅛" in from the leg corner. Glue the strings and ¼" top bands in place, and set overnight.

Leg drops are bought in a background veneer which must be trimmed to desired size and shape. There is always an inlay of some kind bordering the background so this table shows an arrow shape string top and bottom with matching string already placed down the sides. Photo 8-3 shows a jig made to be used with a router collar for these borders. Cut and fit string for these grooves, glue in place, set overnight. Rout out for leg drops (photo 8-4) and trim to string inlay all around.

To make a throwaway pattern of these recesses cover the area with a piece of paper, hold down to keep from shifting, press and slide your thumb along the outline. Cut to crease with scissors, center pattern on inlay and mark outline. Cut close to line with scissors, top and bottom with hand tools. The straight sides can be gradually brought down to size with a hand plane. Mark each insert in case of variation, keeping paper side up. Glue two inserts at a time, one on one leg, one on another. If they should curl out of place, two cross strips of masking tape will keep them from shifting. Cover each inlay with paper, place inlays face to face, position one leg exactly on top of the other, C clamp. Set overnight. (Photo 6-3).

The descriptive steps taken in Chapter 3 and photos 1-8,1-9,1-10,1-12, and 1-13 for oval inlays apply also to this table. The oval shown here is an eagle but any design may be substituted if the overall size will fit the leg (Photo 8-2). Steps to take are as follows: Saw and trim ovals to outline with hand tools, place (with paper side up), and scribe the outline. Use a ¼" router bit to cut close to line, #3

Photo 8-1

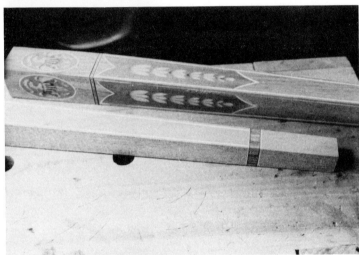

Photo 8-2

Photo 8-3

gouge to trim to line. Fit oval and mark in case of variation. The same gluing procedure is followed as with leg drops, two at a time placed face to face, legs exactly lined up and C clamped.

The remaining inlay work to be done is the ½″ ankle bands. Use the handmade miter box to square cut sixteen banding pieces 1⅛″ long. To start gluing, place one dry piece in a groove, glue the second, butt up to the first, press in place, remove first piece and continue around the leg. Repeat with the remaining three legs. Rough and fine sand all leg surfaces. Glue and place the ¼″ banding in the prepared grooves of the front strip and back skirt, rough and fine sand the outside surfaces of these pieces.

Gluing the frame together will be done in two operations so all joints can be drawn up square and tight. Start with the side skirts. First coat the mortises with glue, then the tenons, put the unit together and lay it on a bar clamp with the inside down because this skirt lines up with the inside leg surfaces and when drawn tight, will bring all shoulders square. Set overnight.

Glue the mortises and tenons of the back skirt and drawer support strip, put it all together with hand pressure, circle the frame with a heavy strap clamp and, before tightening, place the upper drawer strip in position on top of the legs to keep the legs from toeing in when clamped. Try it for square and if necessary put hand pressure on opposite corners to bring it in line. After overnight setting, place the upper drawer strip accurately in position, outline the dovetail shape on each end and rout out to the tail depth, trim to outline with hand tools, coat recesses with glue, press in flush and add a nail for good measure.

The two extra pieces roughed out when making the side skirts can now be used for the leaf supports. On the detail blow-up page this skirt overlay is illustrated. Start with the hinge. About 12″ in from one end, cross cut on a true 90°, set the combination saw to cut 13-16″ high, set fence to leave ⅜″ of wood both top and bottom. End up the 12″ piece, hold the flat side against the cross cut gauge, pass over the saw for one edge, turn to cut the other edge. Reset fence to leave 1½″ of wood, pass over the saw from both edges. The flat sides of the hinge ends of both pieces should be scratched 13-16″ from the ends.

Photo 8-4 shows the end (with the pin inserted) as being the one just worked on. Band saw the waste wood, leaving the ends and center intact. Now carefully set the saw fence to make cuts that will let the two pieces slide together in a neat

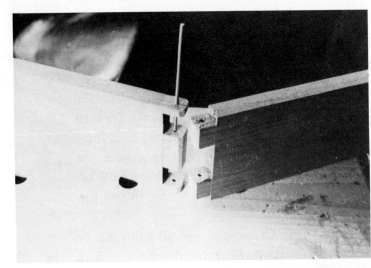

Photo 8-4

Photo 8-5

Photo 8-6

fit. It has been less confusing to speak of one hinge but, of course, two are needed and the same procedure applies for the second one.

The piece shown on the left of photo 8-4 can now be center marked for the 5-32″ wire pin (wire can be procured at any hardware store). Set a scratch gauge to 13-32″ as being one half of the 13-16″ thick support wood, mark the top center and also across the end. The juncture of these lines will be the pinhole center; use an awl to mark for drill. Repeat on the bottom edge. Check the drill press fence for true right-angle and set it to center the 5-32″ drill in an awl mark. Seat the two hinge pieces together and line them up along the fence. Carefully move the work from side to side until the drill is exactly over the awl mark. Slowly drill down the length of the drill, turn over (end for end) and drill from the bottom edge; the two holes should meet in line. Mark the top edge of each piece for the same assembly later; repeat with the other hinge. Plane a ⅛″ flat on each corner so the clearance radius does not have to be too deep.

It will be observed that when the two pieces are put together and a pin entered for trial, the support piece will bind when an attempt is made to swing it; that shows where clearance must be cut. This is not an exacting operation. Use a ½″ chisel, tap with a mallet to sink a V depression about 3-16″ deep in the center of each area. Clearance must be made on both pieces. Cut the pin to 1-16″ more than the length of the hinge, assemble and place, top edge up, on the saw table, enter and tap in the pin. When it stops at the table, peen over the pin top so it will not work its way down when in use. Bring the other support up to this point.

Study photo 8-5 and detail blow-up to see what must be done on the support end. An ogee curve will start 10″ from the hinge pin and swing down in a graceful double curve. There is nothing to match because these two resulting pieces will be kept in their original positions. Square off the end 1″ from the curve line, band saw the curve. Smooth and sand these newly cut edges and gouge out a depression on the back side of the support and on the front or outside of the matching piece. These cuts provide an ample finger hold to swing out the support. (Check with photo 8-5.)

Bore two screw holes through the side skirt to attach the short end piece butted against the front leg, countersink for screw heads because the inside surface of skirt is the border side line for the drawer. Attach end piece. Now place the support curve outline up to its matching counterpart, leaving enough clearance to prevent binding when the support swings out. Mark where the other end must be square cut to butt against the back leg. Square cut to this mark. The need for a V clearance cut in the two hinge pieces also applies to the side skirt where the support corners will move on a radius. Mark where to chisel out for clearance. The longer hinge end should be attached with four countersunk screws for a rigid application. Repeat.

A drawer runner must be attached along each side skirt. The pieces can be ⅝″ square and should border the bottom skirt edge, which will bring it in line with the front drawer strip. These can be fastened with three 1¼″ brads in each.

Cut a drawer front to fit the opening. Because of the curve, use 2″ thick wood (photo 8-6). At each end, on the top edge, make a pencil mark ¾″ forward from the back corner. Insert the piece in the opening, lining up the marks with the front corner of upper drawer strip. Pencil line the strip curve, remove and pencil a line ¾″ back for the drawer front thickness. Instead of continuing the curve to the drawer end, leave about 1¼″ of flat for joining the drawer sides (photo 8-6). Band saw to the back curve but not the front. Plan on making this drawer 22″ deep from front to back. The drawer size needs side, back, and bottom wood ⅜″ thick. (Dovetailing procedure is shown and explained in Chapter 14.) After assembling the drawer, slide it in the opening to check the front pencil line. If it does not match, re-line the front curve and band saw (photo 8-7). Smooth with a spoke shave, rough sand and inlay the front with ¼″ banding (photo 8-5). Insert drawer and glue a stop block on each side.

Depending on facilities, have the rough length 13-16″ boards planed separately or glued together into the required panels and then planed to ¾″. The line drawing shows a quarter section of the full oval laid off in 1″ squares. It calls for the top panel to be 20″ wide but because of possible variation in frame width, make the top exactly 1¼″ wider than the base and 32″ for a rough length. The rough size of the leaf is 13″ wide by 31″ long.

The detail blow-up in conjunction with the thorough instructions in Chapter 4 should furnish all the information necessary to do a good hinge job. Plan on three hinges for each leaf (photo 4-10).

Lay the assembled top unit, bottom side up, pencil in a straight center line the length of the oval and, at right-angles, one across. Place the prepared quarter section on these right-angle lines and pencil the outline. Repeat with the three remaining sections. Band saw, keeping the leaves attached, remove all saw marks

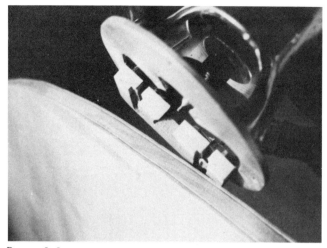

PHOTO 8–7
PHOTO 8–8

from the newly cut outline with a spoke shave, rough sand—using a sandpaper covered block for an even better surface to inlay.

Lay the assembled oval, face side up, on a work table and hand plane any unevenness where leaves meet top; rough sand the entire oval. Now return to the routine string inlaying on the edge. A 1-16″ router bit, fence setting ⅛″ from corner and a depth equal to string thickness, two lines of inlay as photo 8-8 shows. When gluing the strings, seat them right over the top and leaf juncture. Before seating another length, separate the string at top and leaf line with a fine tooth saw. Rough and fine sand the entire border edge.

Usually a router is equipped with a fence having one side in a shallow V shape; this is to be used when working with a convex curve border; if this is not available, one can easily be made. Set the fence for a 1″ border, rout a ⅛″ groove around the oval, glue and seat the inlay, separate at each top and leaf meeting. Coarse sand the inlaid areas, sanding with grain direction. Fine sand the whole oval.

Slope three top fastening screw holes in each side skirt, one in the back and through the front strip at about the center. Turn the base bottom side up. Countersink the front screw hole and, for the others, use a #11 gouge to cut screw head clearance ending in a reasonably good seat ¾″ up for 1¼″ (#7 screws).

Check over the whole table. If any edges or corners feel sharp, smooth with #120 paper. The brass knob will be attached after finishing. For the finishing process read Chapter 15.

9

Round Card Table

MATERIALS

5 leg blanks 1⅝″ x 1⅝″ x 28½″ long

2 pieces 13-16″ x 4″ x 35″ for back skirt and gate

13-16″ wood for top and leaf 9 sq. ft. + waste

15 pieces ⅛″ x 4¼″ x 20″ for curved skirting: 3 of primary wood, 12 of poplar

HARDWARE

1 pair 2″ card table hinges.

INLAY

leg drops (4)

ovals (4)

2 lengths ¼″ banding

1 length ½″ banding

12 lengths 1-16″ stringing

A CARD TABLE is sometimes called a wall table. It can be used any one of three ways: closed, with the leaf flat on the top, against the wall, with the leaf upright or with the gate swung out to support the leaf, making the table a full round for cards or other games.

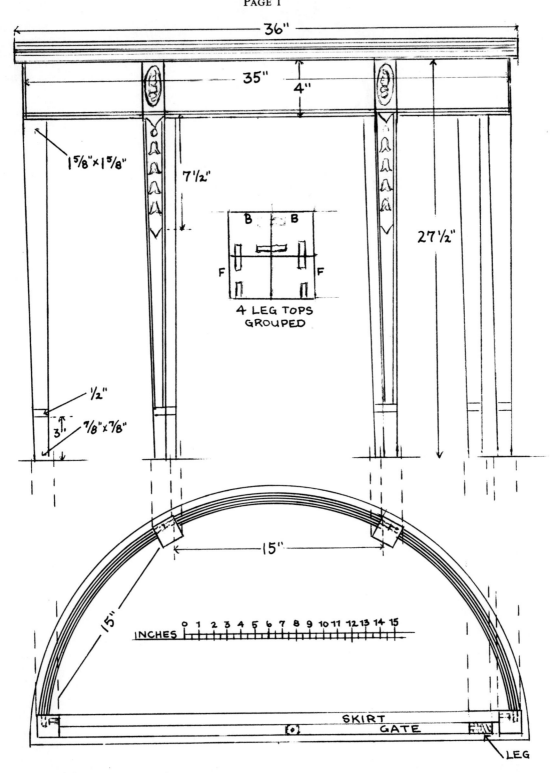

36"

35"

4"

1⁵⁄₈"×1⁵⁄₈"

7¹⁄₂"

27¹⁄₂"

B   B

F   F

4 LEG TOPS
GROUPED

¹⁄₂"

3"

⁷⁄₈"×⁷⁄₈"

15"

15"

INCHES 0 1 2 3 4 5 6 7 8 9 10 11 12 13 14 15

SKIRT

GATE

LEG

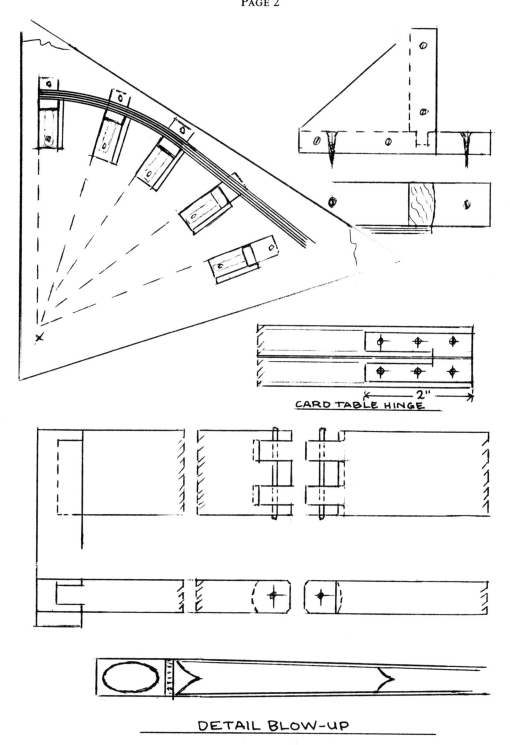

CARD TABLE HINGE

DETAIL BLOW-UP

Making the curved skirting for this table is a process that must be shown and explained as thoroughly as possible. First make the five adjustable form pieces as shown on line drawing blow-up (we will talk about only one for simplicity). The base piece is 8″ long by 2″ wide and may be made of 13-16″ wood (preferably hard). The upright piece is also 13-16″ x 2″ but 5″ in length. On one end of the upright, cut a ⅜″ x ⅜″ tongue. Use the side dado cutters with a ⅜″ spacer between. For the groove, make up the dado for a ⅜″ cut that will be measured 2″ from one end of base piece. Hand plane a slight radius on one 2″ surface that will now be the outside. Glue both tongue and groove, tap in place and pull tight with a C clamp, checking for a true right angle. Set overnight.

For added strength, cut a right-angle piece of ¼″ plywood to fit one side of this assembly (shown on line drawing). Glue the edges of base and upright on the contact area, nail plywood in place with three 1″ nails into each member. A screw hole in each end will complete this unit; five units are needed.

If an old piece of ¾″ plywood large enough to use as a base is available, that will do very well. The radius line to be marked on this base must be determined by stepping down from the 36″ diameter: 18″ top, ½″ overhang = 17½″ less ¾″ thickness of skirt laminate = 16¾″ radius line for the five bending units. If you wish to be extremely accurate, carry the outside surface line of the upright down each side of the 8″ block and place exactly over the 16¾″ radius line on the base. Line up each unit with the center point of the circle, sink two screws in each. Fasten an end one in place, stretch a steel tape across and attach the other end unit 18″ overall. Equalize the other three units in between.

Re-saw the plys that make up the skirt by starting with pieces 13-16″ x 4¼″ x 20″ long. Try to have one surface planed smooth (after each cut run the remaining piece over the jointer). Mount the finest tooth blade that will do the job for as smooth a surface as possible, set the fence for a strong ⅛″ thick ply so that five of them together will measure ¾″ in thickness. The outside ply will be of primary wood, the four inside of poplar. There will be much less chance of breakage across the grain if each set is soaked in water for about two hours, placed in the form wet, clamped, and allow to stand overnight. Then remove and separate to dry (photo 9-1).

Use Weldwood Plastic Resin Glue or the equivalent to bond these pieces. Coat both contacting surfaces when stacking them for clamping. Wooden jaws are ideally suited for the three inside units although not necessary. If iron C clamps are used, put a waste piece of 13-16″ wood under each, sized about 2″ wide by 4″ long, using only one clamp on each unit. Follow the same procedure for two more skirts, (photo 9-2).

Before these laminated skirts are worked on further, rough out the back skirt and the overlay gate assembly. These two pieces may be milled from 13-16″ wood to 4″ wide by 33¼″ finished length. Now, pass one edge of each curved skirt over the jointer to get all five plys even, then saw to the 4″ width. A close tolerance must be maintained on the curved front of these skirts: 15¾″ between shoulders using a steel tape to follow the curve; add to that the ¾″ long tenon on each end. If this measurement varies even ⅛″, the ½″ top overhang will be either too much or too little at the center of the half round. Square off the ends of curved skirts to 17¼″. Make all measurements on the curved fronts.

Set up the dado to make 5-16″ x ¾″ tenons (mortise and tenon procedures have been treated thoroughly in previous chapters). Set the fence for a 5-16″ shoulder on the front. This setting will be used for all tenons except the fifth gate leg. Observe photo 9-3 when running tenons on the curved pieces. (Holding it upright in a 90° position is a matter of eyesight.) After the curved pieces, cut a tenon on each end of the long back skirt. Now, slightly alter the fence to place the tenon in the center of the 13-16″ thickness. This cut is made on one end of the gate piece only.

Remove the waste shoulder wood front and back leaving ¾″ long tenons (photo 9-4). If there is a choice, mark the top edge of each skirt piece and cut away the tenon wood resulting in a ⅜″ shoulder (photo 9-5).

Now process five leg blanks to finished dimensions of 1⅝″ x 1⅝″ x 27½″ long. Tapering legs, and mortising and inlaying them have been treated in Chapters 4, 6, 7, and 8. Photo 6-2 shows a typical mortise operation. The leg shown is one of the back legs and the position of the mortises indicate how the leg is turned: inside back surface up, outside side surface down with the mortise facing the camera provided for the first curved piece forward. There is a slight variation in skirt position on this table: instead of skirt and leg surfaces being flush, the skirts are set back 1-16″. Check the skirt shoulder; if it is 5-16″ then the mortise should be ⅜″ from the front corner. Rough sand the curved skirts.

Photo 9-6 shows a dry assembly, done chiefly to measure the distance from back to front skirt so top overhang will be even all around.

Set up the ¼″ dado for inlay banding groove. Normally the fence would be

Photo 9–1

Photo 9–2

Photo 9–3

set ⅛″ away from the dado to leave a ⅛″ border of the skirt bottom but here the groove must be cut across the legs on the same setting. So the fence must be 3⅞″ from the outside dado cutter. When running the curved skirts over the dado, try to keep the lowest point over the cutter while using a rocking motion to make a more even depth of cut (photo 9-5). Hold the legs against the cross cut gauge to make those grooves, making sure you have the right surfaces. Then make the routine inlay groove cuts, 1-16″ string ⅛″ in from edge, ½″ ankle banding ⅜″ up, four ovals 1⅜″ x 2½″ and the leg drop process explained in Chapter 8 (photos 9-7 and 9-8). Rough and fine sand all leg surfaces, checking all edges to remove sharpness. Coat the walls of mortise and tenon sides with glue, fit the half round frame together, circle it with a strap clamp and draw tight (photo 9-9).

The fifth leg, which presumably has not been mortised, can have a waste block removed 1⅝″ wide by ¾″ thick (from back to front) and 4⅛″ long or high. That should leave about the same measurements standing except ⅞″ thick instead of ¾″. Run a line of mortise holes to place the gate tenon in the center. Straighten the walls and square the ends as with all other mortises (shown on photo 4-5).

Measure and mark from the gate tenon 14″, using the cross cut gauge, make a square cross cut. These will be the two ends for the hinge. Now follow the same procedure as used in Chapter 8 for the hinged support (photo 9-10). The leg may be glued to the hinged gate piece at this time (photo 4-5). Set overnight.

Lay the gate unit on the back skirt leaving about ½″ space between the back corner leg and the gate leg. There is now extra wood to be removed at the other end. A pencil mark on the bottom edge will indicate where to square cut this piece using the cross cut gauge. Photo 9-11 shows the gate assembly which was placed on the back skirt, marked and scooped out for gate clearance. Bore four screw holes for gate unit attachment.

As has been suggested for all larger panels, planing facilities should determine whether or not the individual boards are planed from 13-16″ to ⅝″ or glued together to make up the desired width and then planed. Either way, two panels must be provided to measure 37″ x 19″ each. Rough sand both sides of each panel, look at each side and choose the least attractive surface for the top underside. Place the leaf over the top, lining the back straight edges even with each other. Set a trammel (large compass) to an 18″ radius and draw a half round outline. Clamp the two halves far enough from the ends so they will not interfere with the bandsaw table. Band saw each end on the line for a distance of about 8″ (photo 9-12).

PHOTO 9–4

PHOTO 9–5

PHOTO 9–6

Photo 9-7

Photo 9-8

Photo 9-9

Photo 9-10

Photo 9-11

Photo 9-12

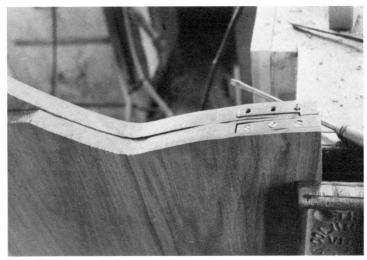

PHOTO 9-13   PHOTO 9-14

The special card table hinges for this piece may be procured from Ball and Ball whose address is listed in the section entitled "Helpful Information." Size to order: 2″.

Separate the two halves. Photo 9-13 shows the table top half with the underside facing the camera, having a hinge cut-out ready for hinge attachment. A router could be used but there would be so much hand tool work besides that it may all be done by hand. The matching leaf end may now be cut for the other half of the hinge. Repeat with the hinge on other end (photo 9-14). Now the rest of the circle can be band sawn (photo 9-12).

Remove all saw marks from the double thickness panels with a spoke shave, rough sand for a uniform radius and groove for two lines of stringing, exactly as described in Chapter 8. After inlaying, coarse and fine sand these edges.

Lay the double top on a work table, top side up. Try to open the two halves; carefully, do not force. They will probably bind, so remove the screws from either hinge half on each end, separate the halves, and round each binding corner but, so not too much wood is removed, connect the panels again for a trial. If binding still takes place, round a little more. Then give it an extra onceover with coarse paper on the top surface and both sides of the leaf before fine sanding. All right-angle corners must be smoothed.

Sloping screw holes for top attachment can be drilled in the skirts about 4″ each way from the back legs and in the center of back skirt and each curved piece. Read Chapter 8 for top attachment. Application of finishing materials is treated in Chapter 15.

10

Chest of Drawers

MATERIALS

2 side panels 13-16″ x 20½″ x 38½″ long

1 top panel ¾″ x 21″ x 41″ long

4 drawer fronts made of one-board widths, 13-16″ thick,
6″, 6¾″, 7″ or 8″ high, and 39″ long

5 drawer division front strips ¾″ x 2″ x 39″ long

About 8 sq. ft. of ¾″ poplar for drawer division frames

About 40 sq. ft. of ½″ poplar for drawer sides, backs, and bottoms

1 piece ¼″ plywood for back 39″ x 32″

INLAY

7 lengths ½″ banding

11 lengths ¼″ banding

5 lengths 1-16″ stringing

HARDWARE

drawer locks (4)

oval escutcheons (4)

oval drawer pulls 3″ boring (8)

CHESTS OF DRAWERS are as basic as tables and chairs in the home. Probably every family could use an extra one or two. This French foot design is a classic that, like good music, never goes out of style.

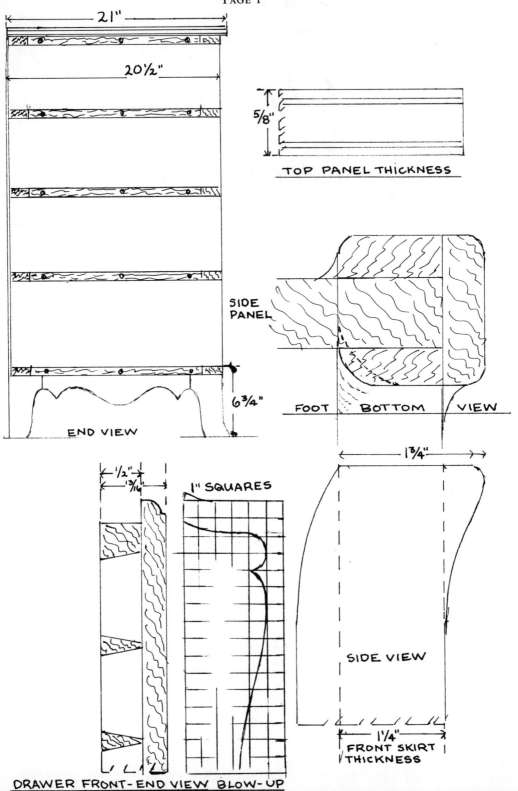

21"

20½"

5/8"

TOP PANEL THICKNESS

SIDE PANEL

6¾"

END VIEW

FOOT   BOTTOM   VIEW

1¾"

½"
13/16"

1" SQUARES

SIDE VIEW

1¼"
FRONT SKIRT
THICKNESS

DRAWER FRONT-END VIEW BLOW-UP

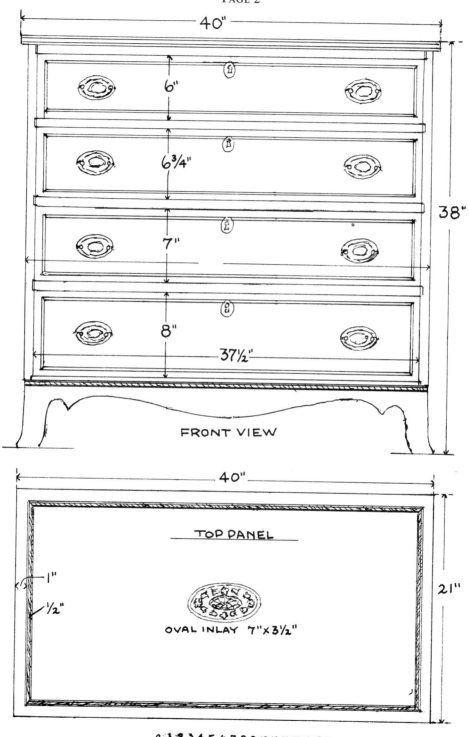

FRONT VIEW

TOP PANEL

OVAL INLAY 7"x3½"

INCHES

Select boards to make up the side panel widths that will leave the least waste. Needed will be two panels 13-16″ thick, 20½″ wide, by a rough length of 38½″.

Glue these boards together to form the two sides. Comments on elementary furniture structuring including joinery can be found in Chapter 15. After gluing, square each panel to 37⅜″ in length, rough sand to smooth any uneven glue joints. Set up the ¾″ dado to cut five division frame grooves ⅛″ deep in each panel (photo 10-1). The top groove starts at the top edge, the next groove to leave a 6″ opening, then 6¾″, 7″, and 8″. The bottom groove can be varied in height to leave 6″ for the feet and skirt. Rabbet the back edges for the ¼″ plywood back panel, making sure the sides will be a pair, right and left. Make the cut ¼″ for plywood thickness and ⅜″ for nailing area.

Also on photo 10-1 a cardboard foot pattern is lying in place. There is no problem in making this pattern: just pencil 1″ squares on a piece of cardboard and draw in the foot line, as shown on line drawing. First place pattern flush with the front edge and outline; then with the back edge and outline. Carefully adjust the two lines to result in a graceful center curve; band saw to these lines.

Five drawer division frames come next. These will be made of ¾″ thick by 2″ wide pieces. Lengths can be determined in this way: the drawing calls for case width of 39″, the side panels are 13-16″ with grooves cut ⅛″ deep. So 39″ less double 11-16″ will indicate a frame length of 37⅝″. Provide five pieces of primary wood ¾″ x 2″ x 37⅝″. Also the same number and size of secondary wood (in this case, poplar). Now determine the depth of frames. Measure from the back rabbet to the front edge which should be 20¼″. Lay a front and back piece side by side and 4″ should be the answer. 20¼″ less 4″ equals 16¼″ plus two ½″ long tongues calls for ten pieces of poplar ¾″ x 2″ x 17¼″ long.

Set up the dado for ¼″ tongues (which are really open end tenons), adjust the fence to place the tongue in the ¾″ thick center. Raise the cutters to ½″ height, mark one side of each short piece with an X so any variation from center will not affect matching tongues to grooves which will also have an X marked on the long pieces. Hold the X's against the fence when milling tongues and grooves. To mill the grooves, remove the ¼″ spacer from the two side dado cutters, raise the dado about 1-16″ higher, adjust the fence to a setting such that, when pressing a short piece against it, the ¼″ cutter will line up exactly with the tongue. Run these grooves about 3″ full depth in from each end of long pieces. Keeping the X against the fence will mean that the end closest to you will have to be lowered onto the saw while pressing against the fence.

Replace the dado with a combination saw and cut away the shoulder wood on both sides to leave ½″ long tongues. Bore three screw holes in the short ends, placed about 1″ in from the tongue shoulder on each end and one in the center. These holes go through the 2″ measurement, not the ¾″. (Screw size is 2½″ x #8.) Gluing can take place now. Coat both tongues and grooves of a frame, press together, place in bar clamps, draw tight, try for square and, if necessary, angle the clamps one way or the other. Leave for fifteen minutes, carefully release clamps, remove and repeat with the next one (photo 10-2).

Probably the drawer locks you will be able to purchase will need a slot ¼″ wide by ¼″ deep by ¼″ back from the front edge of four frames. These are to receive the lock bolts when raised.

Fasten the frames on one side panel with screws flush with the front edge of side panel. Turn over the assembly, place on the other side and fasten (photo 10-3).

As shown on photo 10-4, the feet must be filled in on the inside to permit forming to proper size and shape. Cut four blocks 1¾″ x 1¾″ x 6″ long, temporarily clamp as shown, follow the side shape with a pencil line, place the pattern flush with the corner and mark all the way up the curve until it runs off the block. Band saw to both lines, glue and clamp, set overnight. Repeat.

Before further work is done on the feet, make the front skirt 1¼″ thick by 3″ wide and a neat fit between the blocks glued to the inside surface of the feet; place and temporarily clamp. Lay the pattern on the foot again, continue the pencil line to the end of pattern. Repeat at the other foot end, remove and band saw. Bore three screw holes, one on each end at about the thinnest area and one in the center which must be counterbored to a depth that will leave 2″ for seating a 2½″ screw. For extra rigidity, glue skirt piece when attaching with screws (photo 10-5).

The line drawing shows two views of a foot. The one is from the bottom showing how the flared tips are glued on after being cut to outline. Cut six blocks ½″ thick by 2¼″ wide by 2″ long—one for each back foot and two each for the front. Photo 10-6 shows a block being held on the side surface of a front corner. Hold flush with the front corner and pencil in the back foot line, then band saw.

Photo 10-1

Photo 10-2

Photo 10-3

Photo 10–4

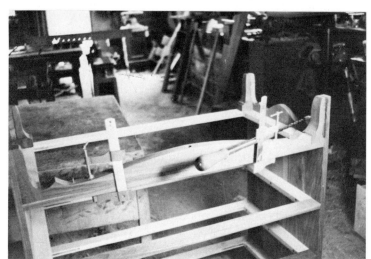

Photo 10–5

Photo 10–6

On this sawed surface, outline the next cut according to the drawing and photo 10-7. After band sawing, keep the waste piece with the good so a reasonably flat surface is provided for clamping. Glue and clamp. Be sure the tip block is not lower than flush because, after setting, the front surface, including the newly glued block, must be hand planed to a smooth level surface for the front block joining (photo 10-8).

Hold the front block in place, being sure a following pencil line will cover the full curve on each side; band saw and mark a side surface with the tip wedge shape outline for the front, band saw. After gluing, a foot should look like photo 10-9. The other front foot should be done the same way. The back feet have only the side block attached because the back corner and surface are simply a straight line.

Before shaping the feet with a spoke shave, set up the router with a ½″ bit, adjust a fence as shown on photo 10-10, clamp a straight edge board so the router will make a cut to cover the skirt joint. Run this groove in depth the thickness of the ½″ banding to be used, follow across each side on the same line, glue in inlay, and set overnight.

Shape the feet with a rounded bed spoke shave. Do the inside right-angle surfaces first. As photo 10-11 shows, after the flat surfaces are smoothed, round the back corner, from very little at the top, tapering to about a 1¾″ radius at the bottom. Sand this back area with coarse and fine paper. The side and front corners can be worked when the case is turned over for side foot finish shaping. The outside side surface shows fairly well on photo 10-11. Round the tip and shave the concave radius to a smooth, even curve, working it down to a feather edge with the side panel. Now the side corner can be rounded from a ¼″ radius at the bottom to practically nothing as it enters the skirt curve. Bring up the back foot to this stage of completion.

Turn the case over end for end and work the feet in like manner. Then turn the case over on its back and shave the front radii like the sides. The remaining corners should be tapered like the side ones, ¼″ radius at the bottom tapered to nothing at the top. Outside foot surfaces will be sanded in conjunction with the case areas.

Sanding large areas such as these case sides, if done by hand, is a long tedious effort but unless one is skillful and with enough back-up experience in the

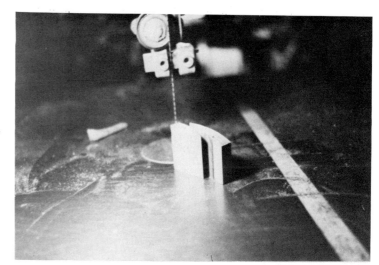

Photo 10–7

Photo 10–8

Photo 10–9

Photo 10–10

Photo 10–11

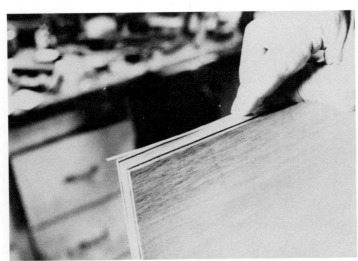

Photo 10–12

use of a portable belt sander it will probably be safer to settle for hand work. Observations relating to sanding can be found in Chapter 15.

The top for this chest could be made of 13-16″ stock lumber but it will be well worth the effort to have the individual boards planed to ⅝″. It is the many seemingly little things including wood thickness that lift one's creation above the average.

Cut enough boards 41″ rough length to make up the 21″ width. When gluing panels this size and no extra width is planned, place two bar clamps on a work table, find two waste strips for the clamp pads to press against, lay the boards on the clamps, shifting them to get the best possible grain match. Set at least one more clamp for top clamping in the center. After board edges are glued, tighten all three clamps to about half the final pressure, use a heavy hammer and a waste block to even all joints, finish tightening the clamps. After overnight setting, rough sand top and bottom surfaces.

Do not try to square off the ends of this panel on the bench saw; it is too wide. Use a large builder's square to draw pencil lines at the 40″ marks and carefully band saw. If these cuts are a little over size, a pass over the jointer will leave a straight, smooth surface. Now follow the routine steps for double line stringing (photo 10-12). After glue setting, coarse and fine sand the front and side edges.

Follow the step-by-step procedure for inlaying ovals treated in Chapters 1, 3, and 5. There may be a sentence or two in each that can furnish a little more enlightenment here. These ovals usually do not lie flat; they may curl or twist, which sometimes makes it difficult to keep them in place for gluing. So the steps to be taken are: remove background up to the oval, pencil a center line the long way on the paper backing and a right-angle line in the center across the oval. Now right-angle lines through the center of the top panel (photo 10-13). Match these lines, oval on top of top panel, hold firmly, scribe an outline, deepen outline with a #3 gouge, rout out close to this line, remove remaining waste wood with hand tools. Photo 10-14 shows the cut-out. Next comes the inlay followed by paper and a ¾″ thick oval slightly larger than the inlay plus a hefty piece of train rail for weight. The only thing missing on this picture is a roll of 1″ masking tape to hold the inlay in place until the other items are added and the weight placed. As mentioned before, glue the recess, fit inlay, strip with tape where necessary, cover with paper, place block directly over inlay and center the weight, setting overnight. Rough sand just enough to remove the paper backing (photo 10-15).

Now insert a border inlay of ½″ banding, set in from the edge one inch. This is another routine operation: set router fence, use ½″ router bit set to the depth of inlay thickness, rout out the groove, square corners with small chisels, miter inlay. There will be another feature added if the ½″ banding is of a decided pattern. There is no need to waste any of the expensive banding, so when the piece used is not long enough and another strip must be added, square cut the new strip where the pattern will continue the end to be matched, and glue in inlay as it is being cut. Rough sand the banding down to the base wood as was done with the oval.

In the top case frame bore top attaching screw holes, three front, three back, and one at center of each end. Front and back holes are placed about 2″ from side panels and one close to the center. Holes bored front and back should be sloped for the driver to clear the lower frame when seating the screws. With end holes sloped inward to clear next frame, use a #11 hand gouge to countersink all holes.

Place top panel upside down on a work table covered with non-scratching material, place the inverted case on the top, measure an overlap of ½″ front and sides, leaving any extra as a back overhang. Use two C clamps front and back to keep the case from creeping when screws are seated. Turn the case upright and do a thorough sand job from start to finish on the whole top area.

Choose the boards for drawer fronts with care. Most furniture parts are fastened to others, which tends to counteract any warpage and twist. In the case of drawer fronts, even a slight twist will cause the drawer to rock on opposite corners. Also, before cutting these fronts, check your cross cut gauge for a true 90° cut. If these cross cuts are out of square (side and back pieces) the completed drawer will rock and bind.

Start by measuring each drawer opening, listing width and height on a piece of scratch paper. A ¼″ lip must be provided for on top and sides but not on the bottom. So, opposite each drawer measurement, enter a new set of figures, adding ¼″ in height and ½″ in width or length of board.

Use the fine tooth 8″ saw to cut the drawer lips. First cut will be made with the fence ½″ from the outside of saw blade and ¼″ in height. Hold the inside drawer front surface against the fence. When the waste wood is removed by the second cut, a ½″ shoulder area will remain (line drawing blow-up). Make this first

PHOTO 10-13

PHOTO 10-14

PHOTO 10-15

PHOTO 10-16

cut on all side and top edges. Re-set the fence to cut ¼″ to the outside of saw blade, raise to cut ½″ in height, cut away the waste wood. Try fitting these drawers. Do not be concerned about height at this time but from side to side there should be about 1-16″ play. If the fit is tight, pass one end over the jointer and again over the saw.

Now for height, hold the front in place at the bottom and if it will not enter the opening at the top, make a jointer cut on the bottom edge, try fit again and, if necessary, repeat jointer cut. Do not run the thumbnail molding on the front corner edges at this time. Drawers of this size need sides, backs, and bottoms of ½″ thick poplar wood (photo 10-16).

Side pieces are to be cut in width (or height) to the drawer front measurement from the bottom edge up to the top shoulder and ½″ less than the distance from the front case corner to the shoulder that will receive the back plywood. The drawer backs should measure the width of drawer fronts between shoulders and ⅝″ less in height.

Set up the two side dado cutters to cut ¼″ x ¼″ grooves for drawer bottoms. Set the fence to cut the top edge of groove ⅝″ above the bottom and, of course, ¼″ deep. Run grooves in all sides and bottom back surface of fronts.

Become familiar with everything that is said in Chapter 14 on dovetailing; it is a key operation in most furniture building. After dovetailing the drawer fronts, they may have the thumbnail molding run on them either with a router bit or on a shaper.

The drawer fronts are decorated with ¼″ banding inlay set ¾″ in from the edge. Proceed as with the banding around the top panel (photo 10-17).

Finally, the locks must be mortised in each drawer front. These are called half mortise locks because only the locking mechanism is imbedded in the wood (photo 10-18). The top edge or selvage is to be cut in flush with the wood, but the back plate is fastened onto the wood surface. The keyhole bored through the front wood is to be the traditional keyhole shape even though it will be covered with an oval escutcheon.

Of course, all drawer parts must be sanded. The drawer front surfaces (with inlay) should be thoroughly sanded, coarse and fine; the same with the molding. Drawer front back surfaces and back surface of the back pieces may be skipped with the sandpaper. All other poplar surfaces may have just a "quickie" #60 grit job.

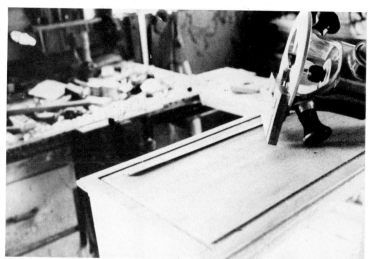

PHOTO 10–17

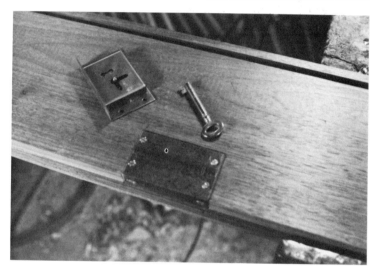

PHOTO 10–18

After carefully going over the whole chest, looking for sharp corners and places that may have been missed with sandpaper, the piece is ready to have the plywood back fitted and nailed in place. Follow Chapter 15 for application of finishing materials. Hardware is fitted as the last operation.

II

Roll-Top Table Desk

MATERIALS

BASE FRAME

4 leg blanks 1½″ x 1½″ x 28½″ long
2 frame side pieces 13-16″ x 3¼″ x 20″ long
1 frame back piece 13-16″ x 3¼″ x 28″ long
2 strips ⅜″ x 1½″ x 28″ long
1 drawer front ⅝″ x 2½″ x 28″ long
poplar wood for drawer ⅜″ thick

DESK UNIT

2 side panels 1⅛″ x 7½″ x 20″ long
1 back frame piece 13-16″ x 4″ x 27″ long
1 front frame piece 13-16″ x 1¾″ x 27″ long
12 roll top pieces ½″ x 13-16″ x 27″ long
writing bed ½″ x 11″ x 27″ long
drawer cover panel ¼″ x 6″ x 27″ long
½″ and ¼″ poplar for interior parts
1 piece of felt (brown or green) 17″ x 27″

INLAY

10 lengths 1-16″ stringing
2 eagle ovals 2″ x 4″
your own make banding and decorative inserts

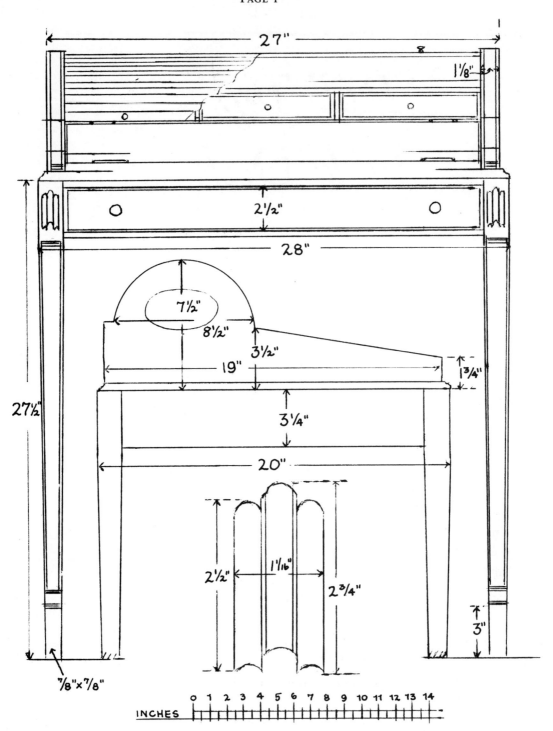

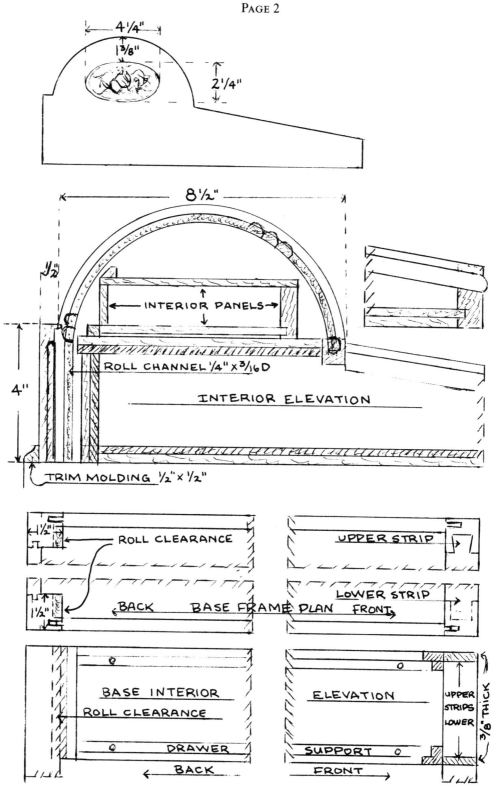

4 1/4"

1 3/8"

2 1/4"

8 1/2"

1/2"

INTERIOR PANELS

ROLL CHANNEL 1/4" X 3/16 D

INTERIOR ELEVATION

4"

TRIM MOLDING 1/2" X 1/2"

1/2"

ROLL CLEARANCE

UPPER STRIP

LOWER STRIP

1/2"

BACK   BASE FRAME PLAN   FRONT

BASE INTERIOR

ROLL CLEARANCE

UPPER
STRIPS
LOWER

3/8" THICK

ELEVATION

DRAWER

SUPPORT

BACK

FRONT

HARDWARE

> ball tip hinges 1¼″ x 1″ (2)
> brass knobs ½″ dia. (2), ¾″ dia. (2), ⅜″ dia. (3)

I WISH I COULD TAKE CREDIT for designing this cute little job but all I did was embellish and alter it here and there for, I hope, even more appeal.

On this desk we will change from the traditional ½″ ankle bands and leg medallions to something that can be made in your own shop. These inlays are to be made of light and dark woods. The best contrast would be dogwood or holly for white, and rosewood for black, but if these are not available, pick the whitest maple and the darkest walnut.

For the tri-bar decoration, take a piece of white wood about 3″ wide by 9″ long, saw to 5-16″ in thickness. It is 9″ long for ease of handling on the saw. Square cut this into three 2½″ lengths, half round one end of each and, using a #7 and #8 gouge, form concave curves on the other ends. A suggestion for making the 1-16″ dark wood dividers between bars is to cut a 3″ wide x 6″ long x 13-16″ thick piece, mount your fine tooth 8″ saw blade, set the fence to cut, not 1-16″ from the fence to the saw but to leave as waste, a 1-16″ veneer strip on the outside of the saw. Cut two 3″ lengths from this strip. Glue all contacting surfaces, assemble as shown on line drawing, with a waste block on each side and tighten two C clamps. Set overnight.

Hand plane the top surface of the glued unit to a smooth flat surface. Set the fence for a smoothing cut on the bottom surface. Waste wood must be removed from the 1-16″ veneer ends, top and bottom, using a fine toothed back saw. Check with line drawing. Re-set the fence to leave, as a waste piece, a 1-16″ thick inlay. Re-set fence and repeat.

For ease of handling, make the 1″ ankle bands about 6″ long. Start with two blocks of white wood about 2″ wide x 6″ long x 13-16″ thick. Saw one of these blocks to ¾″ for the band core. The other one will have, as a waste piece, a 1-16″ veneer sheet sawn from the thick block. Re-set fence and repeat.

Now take a block of dark wood the same size and slice two veneer pieces from it 1-16″ thick. Glue all contacting surfaces, edge up the core piece, place a dark sheet on each side and a white sheet on each outside, add two supporting waste blocks and two C clamps, and set overnight.

Make just one more ⅜" build-up for across the top end of leg stringing and the string ends on the desk unit side panels. Enough waste pieces should be available to provide a white center ⅛" thick, two black 1-16" pieces, and two white 1-16" pieces. Follow the same gluing procedure as with 1" banding. Use either a hand plane or a jointer to smooth one face of these build-ups. Set the fence for slicing procedure, trying to keep all strips not more than 1-16" thick.

Now mill the frame pieces, two sides 13-16" x 3¼" x 18½" long and one back piece 13-16" x 3¼" x 26½" long. Mill two strips for the front, upper and lower, ⅜" x 1½" x 26½" long. Tenons for these frame parts are to be 5-16" x ¾" long. There is really no variation in mortise and tenon procedure from the instructions in Chapters 4 and 8. A 5-16" shoulder is provided on the outside surface so there will be that much wood remaining for strength when the matching mortise will be made in the leg. The 13-16" thickness is divided in this way: 5-16" shoulder, 5-16" tenon, leaving 3-16" for an inside shoulder. Tenons are ¾" long and those cut on the front strips are milled all even with one flat surface, leaving a 1-16" shoulder on one side only. There will be a ⅜" shoulder cut on the top edges of sides and back pieces because the mortises in the legs must start that distance down from the leg top.

Now go through the same tapered leg procedure as was followed in previous chapters: square off 1½" x 1½" leg blanks to 27½", group them in a four square, mark the top ends in pencil where each mortise will be made on the side, marking the fronts with an F. According to the drawing, the legs are tapered to ⅞" so the jointer routine can be employed (photo 11-1).

Grooving for the 1" ankle bands should be done as with ½" banding except that an extra cut in width must be made. Use a ⅝" wide dado set-up with a fence setting at 3"; run the legs. Re-adjust fence for an outside dado cut to match the 1" banding inlay to be used; make second cuts.

Set up the 1-16" router bit for front leg stringing ⅛" in from the edge. These strings will run from the ankle band to exactly 3½" from the top (photo 11-2, which also shows a 3-16" dowel pin going down through the side mortise and tenon). This is often done in frame construction where a heavy superstructure may have considerable usage. Glue stringing in place, set overnight.

Scribe a squared line on the 3½" point from one string to the other, then another for the ⅜" width border band (photo 11-2). Recess this space with hand

Photo 11–1

Photo 11–2

Photo 11–3

chisels, fit a piece of inlay, and glue, using a clamp if necessary. Repeat on the other leg front. Square cut sixteen pieces of 1″ banding 1″ long, glue in, progressing around the legs as described in previous chapters, and set overnight. Rough sand inlaid surfaces down to surrounding wood.

In the upper leg rectangle, center a tri-bar inlay (photo 11-2), hold firmly and scribe around it, making an identifying mark on the inlay and its intended recess. Use hand chisels and gouges to deepen the scribed line. Using a ¼″ router bit adjusted to inlay thickness, rout close to line, finish waste removal with hand tools. Keep shaping the recess until a close fit is accomplished; repeat with the other leg. Glue both cut-outs, press inlays in place, cover each with paper, lay one leg on the other, inlays face to face and clamp, setting overnight.

Coarse and fine sand all leg surfaces. Glue all mortise and tenon joints, putting together the sides first, spanning each side with a bar clamp. Enter the back skirt in its proper mortise, the front lower strip in its socket, turn over this assembly and enter the other end tenons where they belong. Span the already tightened side clamps with two more bars, tighten, check for square and, if necessary, angle these clamps to bring into square, and set overnight.

Place the upper strip in place on top of the front legs, outline with a scriber the dovetail shape on each end, set the router bit to 5-16″ or the thickness of the tail, rout out close to the line (photo 4-6); finish to outline with hand tools, glue sockets, press in the tails, and hammer in a 1″ nail for good measure.

Drill 3-16″ dowel holes into the legs about ¼″ in from the joining line of leg and skirt about ⅞″ deep, cut six lengths of 3-16″ dowel rod about 1″ long, coat holes with glue, tap the dowels in side holes and the same in the back, chisel off excess dowel ends, hand plane any joint unevenness, and sand all newly worked surfaces to a finished condition.

Now look ahead to the situation where the desk unit must be fastened to the base frame. More supporting wood must be provided than is presently there. Since drawer support runners must be attached to the sides, two extra pieces the same size and shape can be inverted and used flush with the top line. The shape of these runners has been described in Chapter 4 but here is a short resume: start with secondary wood 1″ x 1″, cut away the top inside corner, leaving on the bottom a runner surface ⅜″ thick (the strip thickness). Measure the distance from inside surface of side skirt to leg corner to determine the thickness of the side wall. This will leave an L-shaped piece to be cut to fit between front and back legs. Four of them will be needed. Bore two screw holes in each side wall for attaching to side skirts. Two will be attached on the bottom for drawer runners, two inverted and attached at the top edge for desk support. A ⅝″ x ⅝″ strip on the top inside edge of back skirt will complete the supporting wood.

The desk side panels are to be made of 1⅛″ thick wood with an overall size of 7½″ x 19″ long. If a planer is not part of your equipment, you may wish to have two small pieces surfaced at a mill. An alternative is to rough size two pieces of 2″ wood to 4⅛″ x 20″ long and two more 3¾″ x 10″ long. These are narrow enough to re-saw on the circular saw table. Run each piece over the jointer for a smooth starting surface, set the fence for a 1 3-16″ cut, raise the blade to cut mòre than half of the wood width, turn end over end and cut again. Pass the sawn surface over the jointer, taking a 1-16″ deep cut. A square jointer edge cut on each piece will provide for good glue joints. Glue and clamp to produce two panels the shape shown on photo 11-3.

There is no need for an overall pattern for these ends. Square cut the ends to 19″ in length, set a compass for 4¼″ diameter, square a pencil line up the wide end surface 4¾″ from the end. Make a compass center point 3¼″ up this line from the bottom, compass this half circle. Pencil in a ½″ ledge 4″ up on the heavy end (see line drawing), and on the front end of the circle mark a point 3½″ from bottom up. At the front end of panel mark from the bottom 1¾″ up, pencil a straight line between these two points, completing the outline. Photo 11-3 shows one panel band sawn and the other in progress.

Look at the line drawing (Interior Elevation) frequently to check what has to be done. To make the half round roll channel, set up a ¼″ bit in the router, attach a collar to determine what compass radius will be necessary on the follow board (photo 11-4) to leave ¼″ surface wood at the larger radius. Make the follow board as shown on 11-4 with a straight bottom edge and laid off the same as the side panel, i.e. 4¾″ from the left. Make a compass center mark 3¼″ up this line. Now back track with radii measurements, 4¼″ outside, 4″ outer wall of roll groove, 3¾″ inner wall. Now measure accurately how much space there will be between the inner wall and the bearing surface of the collar. Subtract that distance from 3¾″ for the follow board radius. Make the compass half circle and, on the left, square a line up from the bottom to meet it (photo 11-4). On the right side of the

PHOTO 11–4

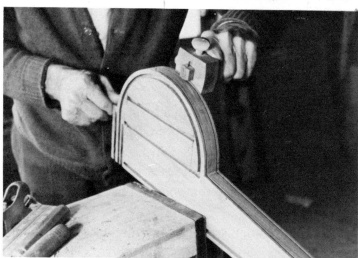

PHOTO 11–5

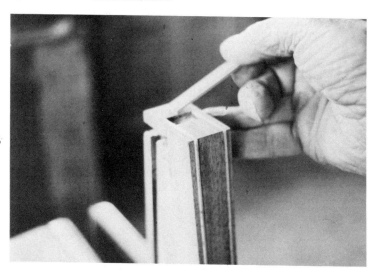

PHOTO 11–6

circle carry the compass line down to a point that will allow the bit to channel ¼″ below the 3½″ point on the side panel.

The walls of these channels should be as smooth and even as possible. To accomplish this, smooth the radius edge of the follow board with a paper-covered block, removing any bumps left by the saw. It may be noticed that the left end of the follow board continues down the squared line and out the bottom edge. This must lead to a continuing clearance in the base for the roll when slid back from the front. The more perfect these channels are the easier the roll will move.

Two of the illustrations can be used to good advantage when making the next series of grooves—the Interior Elevation line drawing and photo 11-5. All of the grooves to be cut in the ends are ¼″ x ¼″ and can be done conveniently on the saw table with the ¼″ dado set-up. Three of these grooves have closed ends but the dado radius left in the ends can be leveled to depth with the router, moving the ¼″ bit free hand.

Before channeling the closed end grooves, make the two vertical grooves in the ends for the 4″ high back board which will be made of 13-16″ stock. These ¼″ wide grooves are ⅝″ deep and set in from the edge 5-16″ to match the planned 5-16″ shoulder to be milled on the back board. That will measure 9-16″ from the edge and should leave about 3-16″ surface wood between this groove and the roll channel. On the other side of the wall channel, leave ½″ of surface wood and run another vertical groove ¼″ x ¼″. Both of these grooves should end 3½″ up from the bottom. The inner groove is for the storage compartment back and is only ½″ thick.

The horizontal grooves can be started with the one for the bottom board which is planned to be flush with the bottom edges of all adjoining parts. That means running the tongue even with the top surface of the ½″ board and the matching groove ¼″ up from the bottom edge. It would be a good idea to look ahead and cut the front frame piece oversize in length and height; that would be a piece of 13-16″ stock 1¼″ wide and 27″ long. Run the bottom groove in this piece at the same time as the sides.

The highest wall of the next higher groove should be ⅛″ less than the 3½″ point where the radius meets the straight sloping line, so the saw fence may be set 3⅛″ to the dado. This groove may join into the roll channel on the front but stop ¼″ from the channel at the back.

The top groove will be placed to leave 1½″ surface wood between the grooves for 1½″ high drawers. This groove must stop ¼″ from roll channel both front and back. Level all groove ends with router (photo 11-5).

An open end mortise for the front frame piece will complete the inside surface of side panels. This piece (which has the bottom groove milled) like the back board will have a ¼″ x ⅝″ long tenon or tongue positioned 5-16″ from the front surface and will require a mortise 5-16″ from the front running from the open bottom 1″ in height as shown on photo 11-6.

The 1⅛″ edge surfaces of the sides should be prepared for inlay by rough sanding to remove any unevenness and deep saw cuts. Because of the curves and inside corners, it is advisable to use the special scratch gauge filed for 1-16″ string grooves instead of the router. The strings will be ⅛″ from the edge and will start ⅝″ up from the bottom, continuing all the way over the top, down the back to within ⅝″ of the bottom. The ⅝″ space, front and back, is to keep the inlay from being covered by the ½″ x ½″ division molding which will be attached as a last operation. The inside corners and abrupt ends of string grooves must be formed with a narrow hand chisel. Glue strings in place and set overnight.

Between the strings, at each end front and back, scratch border lines across for the prepared ⅜″ banding. Use appropriate hand chisels to make the cavity (photo 11-6). Cut, fit, and glue in these border pieces. Sand the inlaid edges to finished condition.

The sides are inlaid with ovals of your choice. Those used here are the same as in Chapter 3 and follow exactly the inlaying procedure for the Card Box. The line drawing shows the oval's position. Coarse and fine sand both surfaces of side panels.

The total width of the desk unit is 27″ so the four interior panels should be made up of boards with a rough length of 27″. Get together all the necessary pieces to complete the unit: a ½″ thick poplar bottom board, the next is also ½″ poplar, and the top is ¼″ primary wood; also ½″ poplar for the vertical back wall inside of the roll channel. Add to these the back and front pieces which have been bottom grooved. All these pieces are to be 24¾″ between shoulders. For each piece add double the length of tenon. Those panels that must be more than 4″ wide will probably have to be made up of two or more pieces. If all drawing measurements have been adhered to, the bottom panel should be 16 7-16″ in width. That figure is determined by the distance from the ¼″ deep front groove to the inner back wall.

Check with the Interior Elevation drawing for the front edge treatment of the next higher panel. Butt hinges will be fastened to this edge so the wood must be heavier here. This panel can be glued up of ½″ poplar, oversize in width, squared off to finished length and the tongues run on it before a piece of primary wood 13-16″ thick by 1¼″ wide is butt joined to the edge, keeping the top surfaces flush. After gluing, each end of the front strip can be squared to shoulder length. As the drawing shows, the finished width of this panel will be from the outside radius point on the front to the rear end of groove.

The ¼″ primary wood panel on top will be the width of the grooves made to receive it. These two pieces being above and below the drawers are the same length so the distance between shoulders can be divided into three equal parts, reducing each section by its share of the two ¼″ vertical drawer division pieces. When this measurement is determined, raise the ¼″ dado to ⅛″ in height, set the fence accordingly, and run these grooves from each end all the way through the top panel but stop 1″ from the front edge of the lower one (photo 11-7).

Glue up pieces of primary wood ¼″ thick by about 4″ long to the width of the top panel. After sanding to a sliding fit in the ¼″ channels, square cut one end, set fence to 1¾″ or the exact measurement needed to keep the panels parallel when inserted into the side grooves.

Presumably the ½″ thick inner back wall piece has had the ¼″ x ¼″ tongues run on the ends with all the shoulder on one side. The width of this piece will be from the under side of second panel to the case bottom edge. Front and back pieces, as mentioned before, have ¼″ x ⅝″ long tenons. The front (already bottom grooved) will be 1″ high at the inner corner and have about a 3″ slope to the front.

The back starts with a 5-16″ shoulder; then a ¼″ tenon takes care of 9-16″ of the 13-16″ thickness. Look carefully at the Interior Elevation drawing to see that the back board should close almost all the opening at the top where the roll will disappear when moved. But that closeness should be only in the form of a lip about ¼″ at the top. As the roll travels down, adequate clearance will be assured if the back is reduced, below the lip, to ⅝″ thickness.

Now check to see what surface areas should be finish sanded before

PHOTO 11-7

PHOTO 11-8

PHOTO 11-9

assembly. The front edge of the second panel up, front edges of two drawer divisions, top and edge surfaces of the top panel, should do it. The interior assembly that surrounds the drawers must be glued together as a unit before complete assembly because the drawer division could not be inserted later (photo 11-7). Having so many parts that must be put together at one time, it will be less exasperating if you make a dry run and ease any tight joints. When gluing, use bar clamps where necessary for a tight fit all around. Check for square.

Make the writing bed next. Glue up ½″ thick pieces to make an oversize panel, allowing for two 2″ wide battens. Measure the opening (side to side) where it will be attached, subtract 4″ for battens, add 1″ for two ½″ long tongues. That will be the exact panel length (photo 11-8).

Mount the dado with a 3-16″ spacer between side cutters, raise to ½″ cutting height, set fence to run these tongues in the middle of the ½″ thickness.

To cut matching grooves in the battens, it will probably be better to use a combination saw and adjust the fence for each of a number of passes. Glue into a single unit, make a straight edge line down one side, band saw, use jointer to smooth the edge. Measure distance from back to front plus 3-16″ for the rounded protrusion on the front (Interior Elevation drawing). Finish sand all surfaces.

About a three-degree angle on the ½″ back edge will bring that surface in parallel line with the panel for hinge attachment. Remove all of the hinge thickness wood from the writing bed, attach hinges to bed, hold bed in place paralleling it with the sides ¼″ down; mark where the hinges must be attached to the panel.

Mill the drawer parts sized to fit the openings—fronts of ½″ thick primary wood; sides, backs, and bottoms ¼″ poplar. Turn to Chapter 14 for complete instructions on dovetailing. There will be a narrow rear ledge in back of the drawers to glue stop blocks. Also the drawing shows a strip about ½″ x ½″ sloped toward the back fastened to the top surface of the top panel to prevent the possibility of papers sliding down in the roll well.

Now for the intriguing feature of this piece, the roll top. Photo 11-9 shows the necessary material for this assembly: ½″ wide strips 13-16″ thick which, after milling, will be parted into two pieces. Also four strips of linen, used because of its strength and lack of bulk.

Twelve of these pieces should be sufficient but an extra one will be a good idea. Round all ½″ sides except one edge which will be used for the front end piece. This leaves a wider flat surface for mounting the two brass knobs.

Photo 11-10 shows one of these wooden strips being rounded on the shaper, both ½″ sides. Now cut to exact length, which is 1-16″ less for clearance than the total span from channel to channel. Finish sand all surfaces and part each piece into two strips ½″ wide by 5-16″ thick (photo 11-11). A large right-angle border must be provided to keep all these strips in a true 90° position when gluing. You may elect to use my method which is to set the fence for one angle and the cross cut gauge for the other. Also, to provide a large enough surface without breaks, place a piece of plywood of any thickness to fit inside this right-angle. Cover the plywood with paper.

So as not to get too far ahead with the gluing, coat each linen tape with glue about 3″ from the end. Position one about 1″ from the fence and one about 1″ from the other end with the last two spaced more or less evenly in between (photo 11-12). Start with the unrounded strip, press down on the tapes, keeping the strip end against the fence and close up to the cross cut gauge. Place the next one against the first, always keeping the ends against the fence. Continue with each successive strip. When necessary, coat another few inches with glue. Caution: these strips *must not* get off the 90° right-angle line. There will be no problem if care is taken when placing each against the preceding one, leaving no space anywhere along the line. Set overnight.

Use a combination saw and set the fence to slightly less than ¼″ width by 3-16″ high, up-end this "rug," keeping the taped side against the fence, pass each end over the saw. Try it in the channels. If it is tight, try to determine if the trouble is in length or if it's a little too thick for the channels. When corrected, the roll should slide in the grooves fairly well—that means a little stiffly but not a real bind. After the channels are coated with finishing materials, the roll will move much more freely.

Photo 11-13 shows the "rug" being inserted in its slot with the front unrounded strip first. Move it over the top to the closed position, mark the last visible strip at the back, and add one more for the total number. Remove any extra strips.

Place the desk unit on the base. There should be an extended border of ½″ all around the base top. Before fastening with screws, try to determine where the

Photo 11-10

Photo 11-11

Photo 11-12

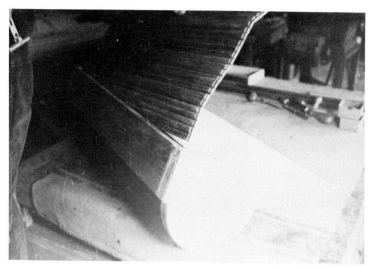

PHOTO 11–13

"rug" will be obstructed when sliding back to open. Probably a certain amount of wood must be removed from the inside corner of each back leg. When the "rug" moves freely, raise the front strip to the radius apex. Glue two stop blocks on the back frame skirt.

Now the desk may be attached to the frame with screws. Before placing in position, bore two screw holes through each of the L-shaped upper strips fastened to frame sides, equalize the border all around, and seat screws up from the bottom.

The division molding should by ½″ high and the width of the ledge running around the desk. This may be of any shape for which cutters are available for either a shaper or a router. Use strips of wood wider than double the molding and run the shape on both sides for better ease of handling and sanding. Finally saw to width, miter, and attach with brads.

Become familiar with finishing techniques discussed in Chapter 15. After finishing materials have been applied, brass knobs can be attached and the bottom board under the writing bed should be covered with felt for a finished appearance.

12

Lady's Desk

MATERIALS

BASE FRAME

4 leg blanks 1⅝″ x 1⅝″ x 26½″ long

2 side skirts 13-16″ x 3⅝″ x 18¾″ long

2 front pieces for upper and lower drawer frames ⅝″ x 1⅝″ x 27″ long

⅝″ poplar wood for drawer frames

DESK UNIT

2 side panels 13-16″ x 8¼″ x 19″ long

1 front piece 13-16″ x 4½″ x 27″ long

1 poplar support piece 13-16″ x 4¾″ x 27″ long

1 poplar drawer support panel ⅝″ x 11″ x 27″ long

½″ poplar for bottom and two halves of writing bed

FLIP WRITING BED

1 panel ½″ x 8½″ x 27″ long

1 piece 13-16″ x 3¼″ x 27″ long

1 piece 13-16″ x 5″ x 27″ long

BOOK CASE

2 side panels 13-16″ x 10¼″ x 21″ long

1 top panel 13-16″ x 10¼″ x 26″ long

1 bottom panel 13-16″ x 10¼″ x 26″ long

1 shelf ⅝″ x 9¾″ x 26″ long

½″ thick wood for doors

2 pieces single thick glass to fit
½″ thick wood for drawer fronts
¼″ thick poplar for drawer backs, sides, and bottoms

INLAY

    6 lengths 1-16″ stringing
    7 lengths ¼″ banding
    3 lengths ⅛″ banding
    2 oval leg fans
    1 large oval 4″ x 7¾″
    ¼″ plywood for backs
    1 piece of felt (brown or green) about 18″ x 27″ for writing bed

HARDWARE

    ivory escutcheons (2)
    clock door locks (2)
    1¼″ broad brass butt hinges (2)
    1″ narrow brass butts (4)
    1¼″ brass knobs (2)
    brass drop drawer pulls (3)

THE DESIGN of this desk is so appealing that it surely should be a "must" for any lady.

If you have made any or all of the preceding pieces of furniture, I like to think that tapering and inlaying legs have become such a common operation that referring to the text is hardly necessary.

The four leg blanks are sized to 1⅝″ x 1⅝″ x 25½″ long. As mentioned before, group the legs into a four square and, on the tops, mark which surfaces will be fronts. On the right angles, mark in pencil a rough mortise shape where they will be placed for side skirts. Also a penciled rabbet ¼″ x ⅜″ for a ¼″ plywood back. Hereafter these legs are rights and lefts.

Interrupt the leg work long enough to mill the side skirts. As the drawing shows, the width is 3⅝″ and the length is figured down from the overall measurement. Start with 18½″, less two legs 3¼″ = 15¼″, plus planned ¾″ tenons = 16¾″ long. Wood for these skirts is 13-16″ thick. Run the ⅜″ x ¾″ long

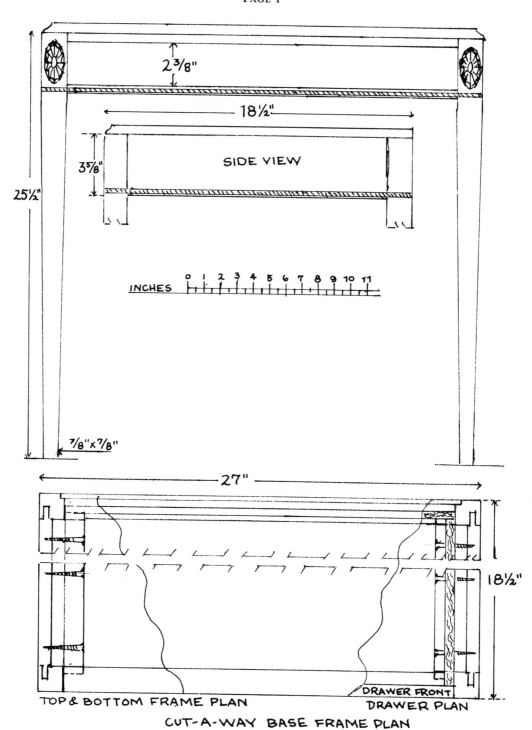

2³⁄₈"

18½"

SIDE VIEW

3⅝"

25½"

INCHES 0 1 2 3 4 5 6 7 8 9 10 11

⁷⁄₈" x ⁷⁄₈"

27"

18½"

TOP & BOTTOM FRAME PLAN

DRAWER FRONT

DRAWER PLAN

CUT-A-WAY BASE FRAME PLAN

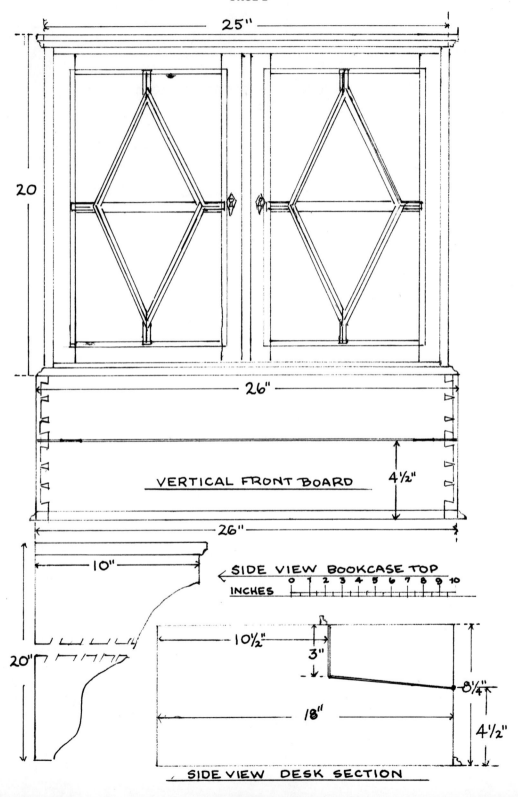

25"

20

26"

VERTICAL FRONT BOARD   4½"

26"

10"

SIDE VIEW BOOKCASE TOP

INCHES   0 1 2 3 4 5 6 7 8 9 10

20"

10½"

3"

8¼"

18"

4½"

SIDE VIEW DESK SECTION

LADY'S DESK
Page 3

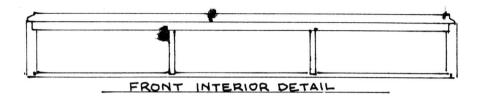

FRONT INTERIOR DETAIL

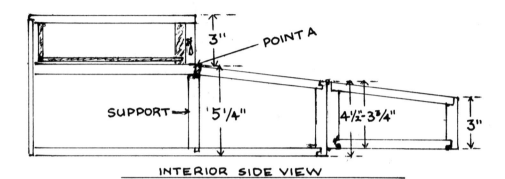

3"

POINT A

SUPPORT → 5 1/4"

4 1/2 - 3 3/4"   3"

INTERIOR SIDE VIEW

DETAIL BLOW-UPS

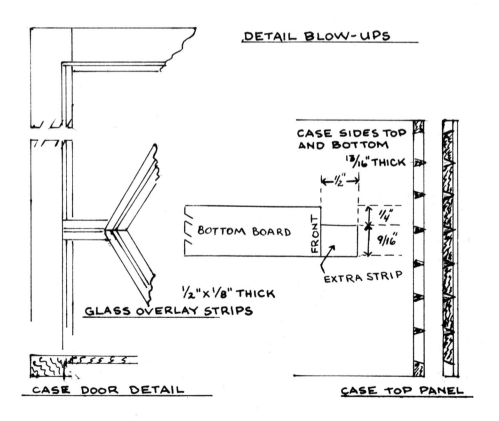

CASE SIDES TOP
AND BOTTOM
1 3/16" THICK

1/2"

BOTTOM BOARD

FRONT

1/4"

9/16"

EXTRA STRIP

1/2" x 1/8" THICK
GLASS OVERLAY STRIPS

CASE DOOR DETAIL

CASE TOP PANEL

tenons leaving a 5-16″ shoulder at the outside corner. Cut away the top of tenons to leave a ⅜″ shoulder. Mortise the legs for these tenons on the pencil-marked surfaces.

So there will be no variation in the drawer opening, set up the ⅝″ dado raised to ⅛″ in height, set fence to cut a groove or rabbet on skirt inside surfaces at the top edge.

Keeping the same fence setting, hold each leg end against the fence and, using the cross cut gauge, make a cut across the predetermined leg surface. Where to place these leg grooves relates directly to the mortises. The best way to be sure is to insert tenons in their proper mortises and make the leg cuts parallel to the skirt rabbet, for both front and back legs. Shift the fence for the far side cutter to 3⅝″, repeat grooving, including legs. When the upper and lower frames are made, fitted, and fastened in these grooves there is no chance of their moving out of position. Taper legs from 1⅝″ to ⅞″.

Inlay two oval fans, centering them as shown on photo 12-1. Instructional details have been treated in preceding chapters. Coarse sand the ovals down to surrounding wood, coarse and fine sand all leg surfaces. Glue coat skirt tenons and mortises, assemble, and draw each side tight with a bar clamp.

Make two ⅝″ thick frames, fronts of primary wood, sides and backs of poplar. Start by determining width and depth. The frame is to be 27″ wide overall so subtract two side skirts but not the full 13-16″. A ⅛″ rabbet was run where these frames will be attached. For total width, figure 27″ less twice 11-16″ or 1⅜″ which leaves a frame width of 25⅝″. In depth measure from the front surface of front leg to the ¼″ rabbet for back panel. The four members of each frame are ripped to these widths—fronts 1⅝″, backs 1⅜″, and sides 2″.

Plan on ¼″ x ½″ long tongues for these frames. The side pieces will therefore be your total distance less 1⅝″ and 1⅜″ plus 1″ for tongues. Square cut all parts to length, set up the dado with a ¼″ spacer, raise to 9-16″, set fence to place tongue in center of ⅝″ thickness. Mark X on one side of all pieces and press the marked side against the fence when making dado cuts. Make the tongue cuts. Use a combination saw to remove shoulder wood ½″ from the end on both sides.

Set up the two side dado cutters, raise to 9-16″; set fence to bring the mortise exactly in line with the tongues. Run the fronts and backs, keeping the X's against the fence. Glue tongues and grooves, lay on two bar clamps and draw tight. Try for square. Bore three screw holes in each side piece (see drawing cut-away) for

2½″ #8 flat head wood screws. Glue tongues and grooves, lay on two bar clamps, and draw tight for square. If adjustment is needed, angle clamps slightly. Set overnight.

After rough sanding over the joints, the frame corners must be notched out to fit around the inside leg corners. The cut-out along the front and back pieces must be the exact measurement of the visible leg surface from the frame groove out to the corner. The right angle (paralleling the side) can be cut to leave about 1-16″ space. Fasten both frames to one side keeping the top surface even with the side top and the fronts even with the front leg surface. Turn the assembly over and attach to the other side (photo 12-2). Rough sand all around, particularly smoothing the surface over all joining member ends.

Set up the ¼″ dado raised to inlay thickness and a fence setting to place the groove ⅛″ from the skirt bottom (photo 12-1). Run this groove across the front and along each side. Coarse and fine sand all around, smooth all sharp corners. This base frame will have a shaky motion until the back panel is nailed in place.

The desk unit starts with two sides 13-16″ x 8¼″ x 18″. The section side view shows all dimensions. When cut to outline, see interior side view. Mill a vertical ¼″ x ¼″ panel groove in the indicated support, continuing groove across the top edge, back to front, and down the sloping front which will receive the poplar writing bed. Cut a ¼″ x ⅜″ rabbet in the vertical back edge to receive the back panel. The groove for ½″ thick poplar bottom should be up ½″ from the bottom edge and run the full length of the sides. Now you're working with right and left panels.

The next panel is in line with point A and should be ⅝″ thick poplar but with the last front piece (making up the necessary width) of primary wood. This three-point intersection is best explained in this manner: the ⅝″ panel top surface should be 1-16″ above point A, and the adjoining writing bed half will be placed 1-16″ below point A. That will bring the bottom surfaces of both panels on an even plane. The 13-16″ thick vertical support will be placed where these two panels meet. Plan on running the ¼″ x ¼″ tongues on the ⅝″ panel ends flush with the top surface. In so doing, there will be only one measurement to keep in mind for the grooves, i.e. 1-16″ above point A.

Grooves for the top and sloping writing bed panels should be milled to receive ¼″ x ¼″ tongues run flush with the bottom surfaces of ½″ thick poplar. The top panel should be even with the top edges of sides but the sloping writing

Photo 12-1

Photo 12-2

Photo 12-3

panel should be lowered 1-16″ from the side panel level. Since these grooves are not parallel with either the top or bottom edges, use the router collar attachment over a ¼″ bit and clamp a follow board to the side panel. Place accurately to bring the groove 9-16″ below the sloping edge. Run through the lower end but stop at point A.

Make ¼″ x ¼″ vertical grooves for the support piece under point A and a ¼″ x ⅜″ rabbet down the back edge of each side panel for a ¼″ plywood back. This will complete the milling on the side pieces.

The common measurement which applies to the length between shoulders of panels and the vertical front board will be 26″ less twice 13-16″ leaving 24⅜″. Add ½″ to this figure for tongues and 1″ for front board dovetails. Where a right-angle joint involving two 13-16″ thick pieces calls for dovetailing, the procedure is explained fully in Chapter 14. The front board, according to the drawing, is 4½″ high and will have a groove for the bottom board ½″ up from the edge and another down from the top to match sides. Widths of these panels will be measured this way: bottom—from front, including tongue, to the rabbet; the ⅝″ panel—from point A to rabbet; the top—from front edge to back edge. Remember that these two top panels are to be faced on the front edge with primary wood.

Three equal openings must be provided for drawers between the top and second down panels but before division pieces are made, the ¼″ x ⅛″ deep grooves should be run for them. Since both panels are the same length, divide that measurement into thirds, allowing for ¼″ tongues on the ends and ¼″ divisions. These channels are to go through the back edge but stop ¾″ from front. Part of that unmarred surface will show because of drawer pull depth.

Coarse and fine sand all exposed surfaces except poplar writing bed which will be only coarse sanded over joints. Remove all sharp corners. Glue tongues, grooves and dovetails, assemble, and use bar clamps where necessary to draw all joints tight. Set overnight.

Measure height of drawer division pieces and, in depth, from the back edge to probably ⅝″ from the front. Remove ⅛″ tongue wood as far back as necessary to fit the groove ends; glue in place. Drawer fronts are to be ½″ thick; sides, backs, and bottoms of ¼″ thick poplar. To determine the depth of drawers, measure the depth of brass drawer pulls plus ⅛″ clearance. That will be the drawer front line, and at the back ⅜″ of support wood should be allowed for stop blocks.

PHOTO 12-4

PHOTO 12-5

PHOTO 12-6

Bore two screw holes through each base frame end piece (front and back) for desk attachment. Place the desk on frame, moving it for ½" border on front and sides. Seat screws from the bottom.

The flip half of the writing bed is a fully enclosed rectangular box with end piece sized to 13-16" thick by 7½" long by 3¾" at one end, tapered to 3" at the other. Measuring for the long sides has already been done for the front board which will be duplicated for these two sides. That measurement was 24⅜" plus 1" for dovetails. One side piece is to be 3¾" wide and the other 3" wide.

Set up the dado for ¼" x ¼" grooves placed to receive ½" thick inside and outside panels with tongues milled flush with the under surfaces. The tapered side pieces should be grooved as a pair. The 7½" tapered edges will be the writing bed side and have the poplar panel 1-16" below the frame edges (photo 12-3).

Dovetail the four corners at this time because you will want a particularly close inside and outside panel fit. Having the tails cut will make it much easier to measure the panel sizes accurately. Consult Chapter 14 for a complete understanding of the procedure.

Both panels are ½" thick. The inside (writing bed half) is made of poplar and the outside of primary wood. After rough sanding the glue joints, square the panels to length, rip to width, and run a ¼" tongue all the way around both. Glue tongues, grooves, and dovetails; assemble and seat the tails firmly with a large hammer and wood block (photo 12-4). Coarse sand the box sides and the outside panel for a smooth, level joining with the frame edges. These joints must be covered with inlay.

Center the oval inlay on the outside surface by following exactly the procedure explained in Chapters 3, 5, and 10. Groove for ¼" banding directly over the panel joint all around, following the Chapter 10 operation (photo 12-5). Coarse and fine sand all surfaces except the writing bed.

Look at photos 12-6 and 12-7 to see what must be done for a smooth level writing bed over the hinged joint. Both desk half and the flip half have a 1-16" raised edge all around so the sides that come together must have those raised edges spoke-shaved flush with the panels. Rout out to a depth equal to the hinge plate thickness for the two broad brass butts placed up to the raised edge on each side (photos 12-6, 12-7, 12-8).

The book case top is not too complicated to make. The drawing calls for sides 13-16″ x 10″ x 20″ long (or high). Top and bottom 13-16″ x 10″ x 23⅜″ between shoulders plus 1″ for dovetails = 24⅜″.

A shelf ⅝″ thick can be sized after the case is assembled. Because of the ½″ x 1″ molding around the top, an extra strip 13-16″ square must be glued to the under side of the top panel to extend the face surface below the molding. This extra strip is needed now to have the ½″ x ¼″ rabbet milled at the same time as the sides. The ½″ deep rabbet is to provide a ¼″ shoulder seat for the ½″ doors. Sand all rabbet surfaces.

Make these rabbets on the sides and top strip front edges but not the bottom. It will be easier to glue a strip 9-16″ x ½″ to the bottom forming a matching rabbet to the sides, closing side channel ends, see detail blow-up.

Shelf grooves ⅝″ wide by ¼″ deep should be made at this time. They must be measured to be centered in the opening of the completed case, which means the extra top strip must be considered. Also a rabbet must be cut ¼″ x ⅜″ for the ¼″ plywood back; these cuts are to be made on the back edges of all four pieces.

Follow dovetailing instructions in Chapter 14 for joining two pieces 13-16″ thick (photos 12-9 and 12-10). Because the bottom panel will be ½″ less in width, lay off the dovetails from the back edges.

After coarse and fine sanding of the four inside surfaces, the case may be assembled by gluing the tails, fitting the parts together, and using a hammer and block to seat tightly. Try for square. Now fit the extra top strip to cover the unwanted ends of side channels, then glue to the under side of the top panel. Saw a strip to form the bottom rabbet, ½″ thick by 9-16″ wide and in length to fit between side walls. Glue to front edge of bottom panel.

Size a door division strip to ½″ wide x ¾″ deep, cut to fit between top and bottom rabbet. It will be necessary to make open end mortises ¼″ deep and ½″ wide so the strip will fit flush with the front surface. This division piece will, of course, be centered vertically. Coarse and fine sand all outside surfaces except the bottom.

The top molding is a simple strip ½″ thick by 1″ wide (or high) with the outer lower corner cut into a cove. Using the router cutter, miter corners and, after sanding, glue and brad in place.

The doors are made of ½″ x 1¼″ pieces cut in length to fit the opening, both vertical and horizontal. Tongues on the cross pieces will be too long to use the

Photo 12-7

Photo 12-8

Photo 12-9

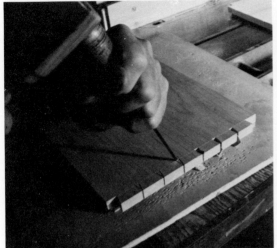

Photo 12–10

Photo 12–11

Photo 12–12

Photo 12–13

Photo 12–14

dado so a combination saw blade will serve. After cutting to length, mark an X on one side of each piece and when performing each operation, press the X side against the fence. Portion out the ½″ thickness into three parts after reducing it to 1-32″; therefore the tongues will be about 5-32″ leaving about the same thickness of shoulder wood on each side for the grooved piece.

Raise the saw blade to cut 1¼″ in height, set the fence 5-32″ to the outside of the blade, upend a cross piece with the X toward the fence, pass it over the saw, repeat all short pieces. Re-set the fence to make the next cut about 10-32″ to the inside of saw. Run all short ends.

Lower saw and set the fence to remove shoulder wood on each side 1¼″ from ends, using the cross cut gauge for this operation.

Raise the saw again to 1¼″ high, bring the fence in close, hold a tenoned piece (X against fence), adjust the fence to a probable first groove cut, run through a piece of scrap and compare with tenon. Since this is scrap, remove all the outside wood and lay the remainder on a tenon to see that the two surfaces are flush; if necessary, make adjustment. Run the long pieces. Before readjusting the fence, run another piece of scrap to use for the next cuts. Re-set fence, make a narrow cut on the scrap, making sure the groove is not too wide. Run the good pieces and continue until a neat fit is achieved (photo 12-11). Glue tenons and grooves, lay frame on two bar clamps with two more clamps at right angle on top; gradually tighten two at a time until all joints are pulled up satisfactorily. Immediately remove from clamps and try fit in its opening; if necessary, spring it slightly by hand to adjust. Repeat with the other frame.

After sanding all joints flush, insert a ¼″ or larger bit in the router, adjust to 5-16″ deep, and set the fence to leave 1″ of surface wood. That will result in a ¼″ x 5-16″ deep rabbet for the glass. Square out corners with hand tools and repeat (photo 12-12).

Using a 1-16″ router bit set for inlay stringing, groove ¼″ from the inner edge of doors all around. Have the fence bear against the outside edge (photo 12-13).

Half mortise in the two style I clock door locks (obtainable from Ball and Ball). Inlay the ivory keyhole escutcheons (photo 12-14). Cut out half the 1″ butt thickness to hang the doors about 1½″ from top and bottom. Make matching cuts for the other hinge half in the case frame (photo 12-15).

Now make the glass overlay strips. Start with a variable width piece sawn to ½" thickness. On one edge (photo 12-16) rout a 1-16" string groove down the middle, glue in the inlay and, when set, sand smooth. With a fine tooth saw, slice off a 3-16" thick strip (this should equal exactly the lip thickness over the glass). Make enough lengths for the diamond overlay work. Make neat fit cut-outs, centered on each inside edge for these diamond strip pieces. Cut-outs will be ½" wide and extend into the string inlay (photo 12-13). Do not proceed any further with the strips until finishing materials have been applied, including the strip lengths.

Bore two screw holes through the case bottom, placed about 3" from the sides and about center from front to back. Countersink with a gouge inside. Place the case in position on the desk top, equalize the border, front and sides; seat screws. Now use a simple ogee or whatever molding cutter you may have for the router. These division strips will be ½" x ½" and, after molding and sanding, miter corners and fasten with brads into the desk (not the book case).

The ¼" plywood backs should be fitted with care, especially the one-piece back to cover both the base frame and the desk. This panel, when nailed in, will give the piece needed side rigidity. Cut, fit, and nail in the book case back.

Go over all surfaces, looking for any places that may have been missed with sandpaper. Feel for sharp corners and remove with folded #120 grit paper.

Separate the desk and book case top, remove the flip writing bed for finishing. Apply finishing materials to the whole piece (except the poplar writing bed), following instructions in Chapter 15.

Cover a work table with non-scratching material, lay a door face down, fit a pre-cut piece of glass in place and fasten with strips about 3-16" square, using ½" brads. Flip the door over and cut the overlay pieces starting with the ones extending at right angles from the frame. Make those short pieces a uniform 1½" in length. After the short pieces are fitted in place lay a long strip over two of them for one diamond side, pencil in where to saw for length and angle. Have all pieces fitted before gluing. Use Weldwood Contact Cement or its equivalent. Do not be careless with the cement; a narrow band running the length of each piece down the center and a spot on each joining end should be sufficient.

Attach the flip writing box in place again, squeeze a line of Elmer's or equivalent glue all around the edge for felt contact. Also put a line of glue on each side of the hinge joining line. Press the felt in place, smoothing out all

PHOTO 12-15

PHOTO 12-16

PHOTO 12-17

wrinkles and stretching as much as possible by hand. Leave overnight (photo 12-8).

Use a sharp razor blade to part the felt on the border line and neatly uncover the hinge rolls (photo 12-17). Also part the felt into two halves on the hinge line because there will be a varying space between these joints as the bed is closed. Bore for and attach hardware as an end to your work.

13

Slope-Top Desk

MATERIALS

    2 side panels 13-16″ x 20″ x 41″ long

    1 top panel 13-16″ x 11″ x 41″ long

    1 writing bed 13-16″ x 20″ x 40″ long

    1 writing leaf 13-16″ x 15″ x 38″ long

    4 drawer fronts 13-16″ x 4″ x 40″ long, 13-16″ x 4¾″ x 40″ long,
       13-16″ x 5½″ x 40″ long, and 13-16″ x 6″ x 40″ long

  wood for 4 drawer division frames, the fronts of
     primary wood, the rest poplar ¾″ thick

  4 blocks 2″ x 2″ x 5½″ long

  1 base pigeonhole panel ⅜″ x 11″ x 40″

  small drawer fronts of ½″ wood

  ¼″ poplar for sides, backs, and bottoms. Most other wood for pigeonhole is
     ¼″ thick.

  Large drawers require ½″ poplar for sides, backs, and bottoms.

  1 back panel ¼″ plywood 36″ x 40″

INLAY

    3 lengths ½″ banding

    11 lengths ¼″ banding

    10 lengths 1-16″ stringing

    1 small oval 1¼″ x 3″

    1 large oval 3″ x 7″

HARDWARE

    oval drawer pulls 3″ boring (8)
    ¾″ diameter knobs (2)
    ½″ diameter knobs (8)
    1″ narrow brass butts (2)
    1½″ desk hinges (sometimes called broad brass butts) (3)
    drawer locks (4)
    desk lock (Ball and Ball) (1)
    clock door lock (Ball and Ball) (1)
    ivory escutcheons (5)

IF YOU HAVE MADE any or all of the masterpieces up to this chapter, you really do deserve to have one you can call your very own. What could be a better selection than this Slope-Top Desk. For the living room, it will be a piece to look at and use with pride for the rest of your life, and then some, so let's make it "super."

Up to the writing bed there is very little difference between this desk and the chest of drawers in Chapter 10. Start with the familiar routine of random width 13-16″ boards to make up side panels 20″ wide by 41″ long. Level all joints with a hand plane; coarse sand both sides. Square ends to 40″ in length.

The side interior shows where to lay off for ¾″ drawer division frames. Start at the bottom, measure up 5½″ for the feet, then ¾″ for the first frame; after that, 6″ for the bottom drawer, ¾″ for the next frame, then 5½″, ¾″, 4¾″, ¾″, 4″, then 13-16″ for the writing bed. That totals 29 9-16″ to point A. Above the groove at point A, measure 4 11-16″ to the first ¼″ small drawer support groove, then 2¼″ for the drawer, ¼″ again and 2¼″ for the top drawer. This should leave 13-16″ to the squared off top edge. If there is any variation, take it up in the 4 11-16″ space.

Set up the dado for ¾″ wide, raised to ⅛″ high, set the fence for the first groove, cut the full width, work the two sides at the same time. Move to the next higher groove and on up to the writing bed which will be 13-16″ wide and 13-16″ deep. Now choose and mark the edge of each panel for the back. They are now a pair, right and left. Move up to the ¼″ wide x 3-16″ deep short grooves, cut through the back edge and stop 9¾″ toward the front. Square out the groove ends with hand tools. Photo 13-1 shows all grooves cut and the sloping front edge marked for band sawing.

SLOPE-TOP DESK

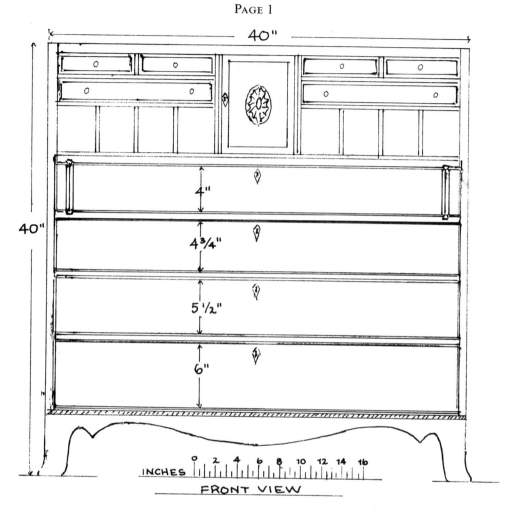

FRONT VIEW

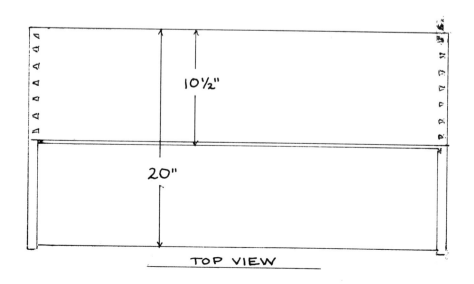

TOP VIEW

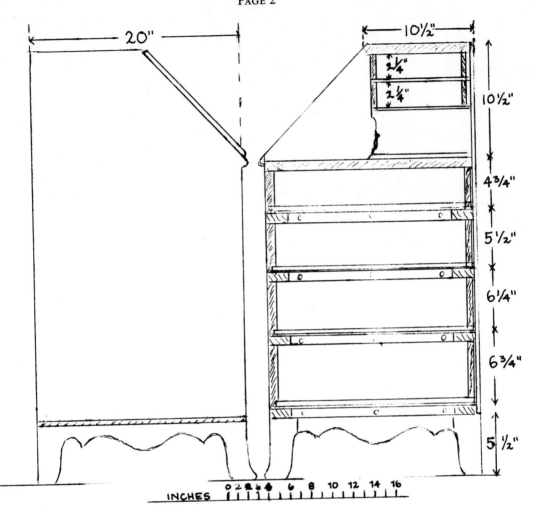

20"

10½"

2¼"

2¼"

10½"

4¾"

5½"

6¼"

6¾"

5½"

INCHES 0 2 4 6 8 10 12 14 16

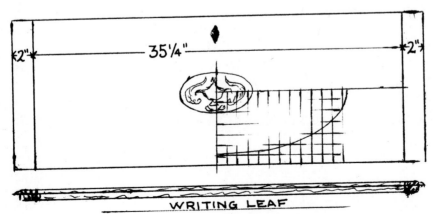

2" 35¼" 2"

WRITING LEAF

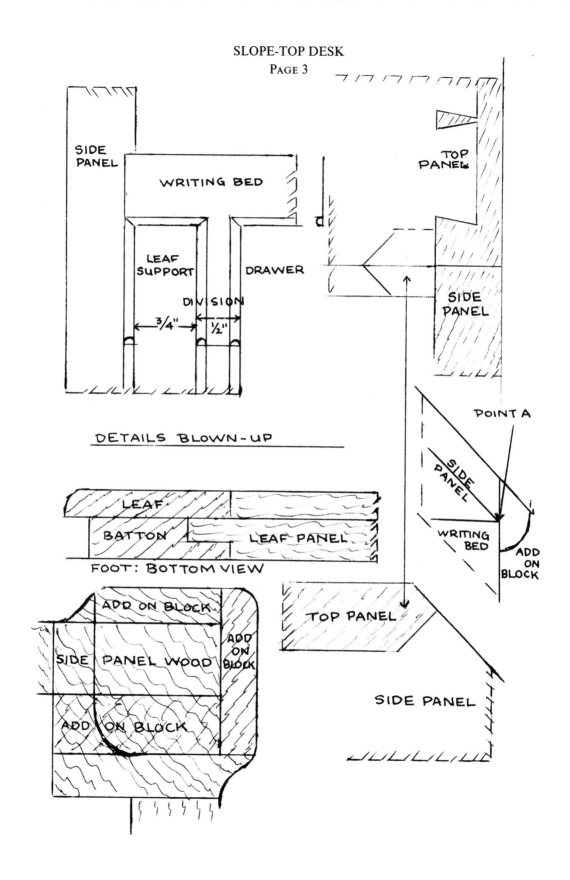

SIDE PANEL

WRITING BED

LEAF SUPPORT

DRAWER

DIVISION

3/4" 1/2"

TOP PANEL

SIDE PANEL

POINT A

SIDE PANEL

WRITING BED

ADD ON BLOCK

DETAILS BLOWN-UP

LEAF

BATTON

LEAF PANEL

FOOT: BOTTOM VIEW

ADD ON BLOCK

SIDE PANEL WOOD

ADD ON BLOCK

ADD ON BLOCK

TOP PANEL

SIDE PANEL

Contrary to what you might expect, this sloping line must not be marked from the full top panel width to point A at the writing bed. The widest point of the top panel is down about one half of the top thickness (see blow-up drawing) and the lower end must provide for the 7-16″ deep rabbet around the lid. Make a pencil dot about ⅜″ down from the top edge and 10½″ from the back. On the front edge make a dot ⅝″ above point A. Use a straight edge to mark from point to point. A rabbet along each back edge for ¼″ plywood ⅜″ wide will finish milling on the sides for the time being.

Cut the dovetails for the top panel even though the top has not been glued and sized. The reason: a much more accurate length can be determined after the case has been assembled with division frames in place. These tails are marked with the same templates as large drawer fronts. Follow instructions in Chapter 14 and study photos 13-2 and 13-3.

Drawer division frames can be made next. They are like those on the chest of drawers in Chapter ten. Use wood ¾″ thick, 2″ wide, and 38⅝″ long for front and back pieces. The side pieces are measured to make the complete frame size reach from back rabbet to front edge. Sides and back pieces are of poplar; tongues are ¼″ x ½″ long.

The writing bed is to be the same width as the frames and since only the back half will be covered, that part may be made of poplar.

Photo 13-4 shows particularly well the bead that borders all the larger drawer openings. How these beads will be formed depends upon the equipment available. The best method is to have a specially ground shaper cutter but in lieu of that, possibly a router set-up could be arranged. It may be necessary to fall back on the simple dado set-up, where a bead on each edge of a frame is left raised when the ½″ dado removes the wood between. Of course these raised edges are not beads at this point. Make a sanding block for this purpose by edging up a ¼″ thick wood piece, carving a shallow half round channel about 3-16″ wide by ⅛″ deep along its length, cover its working edge with #60 grit paper and sand the bead's square corners to a half round contour.

As has been noted, the intermediate division frames need the two beads but the writing bed has but one on the lower edge and the bottom frame has one on the upper edge. The side panels have only one on the inside corner of each. That leaves just two more parts to be beaded: the vertical separating strips between the

Photo 13-1

Photo 13-2

Photo 13-3

top drawer and the leaf supports, which can be done when made and fitted (see drawing blow-up).

Dado a ½″ wide x 3-16″ deep groove from front to back on each end of the top division frame for the separating strips. These are measured in from the ends ⅛″ for side panel channel plus ¾″ for support so a fence setting ⅞″ is indicated. Do not try to make the matching groove on the under side of writing bed at this time, because the chances of getting a perfectly parallel line with the side panels are slim indeed. After assembly, the upper grooves can be carefully marked and cut by hand. A ¼″ dado cut ¼″ deep can be made for drawer lock bolts above each drawer. Unlike the chest in Chapter 10 which has lip drawers, these grooves should be placed 9-16″ back from the front edges.

Check to see if everything is ready for assembly. Make three screw holes through frame ends. Inside surfaces of side panels above the writing bed must be finish sanded, also the exposed portion of the writing bed.

Fasten the four frames in their grooves on one side panel with 2½″ #8 screws, turn over the partial assembly, seat frames in the other side grooves, sink screws. Do not try to position writing bed now. There will be much less stress throughout the whole case if this panel placement is delayed until the top is dovetailed and seated.

The tails have been cut for the top panel so an accurate length measurement can be made for the top board. To determine what this figure will be, measure the distance from inside side surface to inside side surface at the top frame line. The corresponding measuring points up at the dovetail area should be exactly the same; if not, use a bar clamp to pull in or a waste stick to force out. Now measure the total length required for the top panel. Cut away waste shoulder wood to leave end extensions ½″ thick and ½″ long (study photos 13-2 and 13-3).

Marking for the female cuts is the same as for a drawer side, holding the template at the matching back edge as was done with the side panels.

A pigeonhole base panel must be made now because matching grooves are to be cut in top and base for the two ½″ thick side wall panels which will border the interior door. The base panel should measure ⅜″ thick, 9¾″ wide, and exactly the same length as the top board. It will have to be cut and fitted to length after matching grooves have been cut.

Set up the ¼″ dado raised to 3-16″ in height, set the fence to leave 7″

between when the grooves are run from each end. Grooves in the top will end 9¾″ from the back edge or 9½″ from the back rabbet. Run the base panel all the way from back to front on the same fence set-up. Mark on the top underside, working toward the end, where a ½″ thick wall panel will be placed. The panel tongue will be run on the 7″ or inside surface so a pencil mark ¼″ past the groove will be the point to measure to the dovetail shoulder. Half of that distance will be the center of the next groove in the top only.

In case the rabbet for the back panel has not been made, run it now, ¼″ deep and ⅜″ wide. Also make the right-angle point on the front edge. This can be done easily by tilting the jointer fence to 45°. Before sanding and gluing in place, level out all four groove ends with a ¼″ router bit. Sand to finish condition the front edges and the top underside in the area of the center door, glue the tails, lower top in place and use a block and large hammer to seat tightly.

Now the writing bed must be made to slide in its grooves without too much force. It is usually better to work from the back so any possible marks will be on the back edge. Check the bed length for a neat but not tight fit. Start the bed in the grooves; if and when it becomes tight, withdraw and hand plane the bottom surface at the ends, and try again. When you believe it will go the whole way, withdraw and coat the grooves with glue, enter it, push as far as possible by hand, then use a block and large hammer, first a little on one end and then on the other. When flush with the front, seat a #16 1¼″ brad in the corner near the back on an angle that will bring the brad well into the side panel wood; repeat on other end.

Turn the case upside down, mark exactly where the separating division channel will be cut. Use a fine-toothed back saw to cut farther in than is necessary for insertion of a piece ½″ thick by 1¼″ wide, channels to be 3-16″ deep. Before cutting to length, bead both corners of one edge (photo 13-4). Cut two lengths, glue channels, and insert flush with the front.

It was not mentioned specifically whether or not to build up the feet at the time of frame fastening. If this operation was not worked on, the complete instructions for the chest of drawers, Chapter 10, can be followed exactly. As a supplement to the information furnished in Chapter 10, there are different photo views (13-5, 13-6, and 13-7) plus a slightly different presentation on the line drawing page for this chapter. The instructions followed include the ½″ band inlay that covers the skirt and bottom frame joint.

PHOTO 13-4

PHOTO 13-5

PHOTO 13-6

Turn the case upright on its feet, make two poplar pieces to fill the ½″ grooves that run to the back from the vertical separating strips. These pieces will fit the ½″ grooves and be about 1½″ high, and even with the frame in the back. These pieces should be a tight enough fit so that, when glued, no other fastening devices are necessary (photo 13-4).

The beads surrounding all drawer openings can be worked on with hand tools to make the corners look as much like miters as possible. It may be necessary in places to burn in some stick shellac. Remove the unwanted side bead at the writing bed juncture, work the area to a level surface for gluing the "add on" radius block. When set, this block will form an extension of the sloping side line which can now be hand planed to remove saw marks and level out the top and side juncture surfaces. The rabbets provided for the back board come through the top end of the sides and must have little fill-in blocks fitted and glued in place, keeping the same grain direction as side wood.

Hand plane over the top dovetails to leave a smooth surface for coarse and fine sanding of the whole top. Tip the case over on one side, coarse and fine sand, turn over to do the other side.

Now work on the interior or pigeonhole. All the panels that make up this structure are 9½″ wide, or deep. Fit the base panel in place by sawing *exactly* the same amount of wood from each end; that will keep the center grooves perpendicular with the top ones. Divide the distance from groove to the end into four parts, run three ¼″ wide by ⅛″ deep grooves from front to back, repeat on other end, sand edge and the area between center grooves, place it in position and use about four 1″ brads near the back to anchor it.

Two ½″ thick door rectangle sides are to be made next. They will measure 9½″ wide by the full depth of grooves in height; run ¼″ x 3-16″ long tongues on ends keeping all of the shoulders on one side. Use a scratch gauge to make a deep line down the center of the front ½″ surface, and use a wedge-shaped block covered with paper to round the two halves into beads. Work the two at the same time. Choose one for the right side, place 1″ hinges one inch from the ends on the inside surface leaving the pin roll to extend past the panel edge. Scribe a line around the half hinge, set a router bit to cut half of the hinge thickness, square out with hand tools (photo 13-8). Make sure the sides are a pair (right and left) in relation to the tongues.

PHOTO 13-7

PHOTO 13-8

PHOTO 13-9

Insert the sides a short distance from the back, pencil a line at the right angle where the tongue enters the groove. Do this on both panels. Measure from the corresponding corner at the top end, down to the first groove; mark this distance down from the pencil line on sides; repeat for the next groove. Sand both sides of side panels, glue grooves, and position with the front edges flush with the base (photo 13-9).

Provide four small drawer support panels, ¼″ thick by 9½″ by groove to groove in length (photo 13-10). The upper ones may be made of poplar with just a facing strip of primary wood. Slide all four in place and, as can be seen on photo 13-10, grooves must be cut to match those in the top and three each side on the base. The best way to be sure of each division piece being perpendicular is to saw a waste block into a true right angle on one end. Make this block about the height of the lower opening and use it as a small square. Place it at one side of a groove, mark under the drawer support, move to the other groove side and mark again; repeat with all grooves. Saw the block's height to fit in the upper opening; repeat the marking.

Set up ¼″ dado ⅛″ deep, use the fence and cross cut gauge to cross cut between pencil marks, sand front edges, glue grooves, slide in panels flush with the front line. Make up all division pieces with vertical grain. These are so small that clamping is impractical. Try just rub joining, coat one edge with glue while holding the other in a vise, slide gently back and forth, keeping the surfaces even, until you feel the glue taking hold, then release hands gently. Allow about an hour before adding another piece.

Cut these pieces 9½″ wide by a length to fit. Do not have them too long or they will bow the grooved panels. Pigeonhole division should have the double ogee jig sawed on the front edges, rounded slightly with sandpaper. Coarse and fine sand the surfaces, spot glue the grooves, slide all pieces in place, flush on the front.

Make up an interior door ⅝″ thick and sized to fit in its opening; coarse sand all surfaces. Wedge it in the opening with a bottom shim. Needlepoint a dot to show where to cut for each hinge. Place each hinge between points with roll extended, scribe a border line, rout and square corners with hand tools, fasten hinges, try for clearance, remove and hand plane if and where necessary.

Inlaying ovals has been explained in detail in previous chapters so more said

Photo 13-10

Photo 13-11

Photo 13-12

on the subject would be superfluous. The oval fan is placed in the center of door panel and 1-16″ stringing ½″ from the edge all around (photo 13-11). Mortise in the clock door lock as explained in Chapter 12 and inlay an ivory escutcheon. Coarse sand the inlaid surface and fine sand all door surfaces. When the door is again mounted, glue and brad a 3-16″ x 3-16″ strip from top to bottom on the left side for a door stop.

Two leaf supports should be made next. They must be sized to slide easily in the channels provided and of such length that they end ½″ from the back rabbets. That space is for nailed-on stop blocks. After sanding, recess the front surfaces 1-16″ of the thickness of the half beads and apply blocks (photo 13-12). Pull out the supports 9″ and fasten stop blocks in back of the front separating strips, one screw in each but no glue because these supports must be removed for finishing (photo 13-4).

Measure the lid or writing leaf opening, in length from side to side and width from the top point to the writing bed top corner. Plan on a 5-16″ lip (like a lipped drawer front) on each side and the top edge but not the bottom. Add to the opening size ⅝″ in length and 5-16″ in width. The lid will have a 2″ wide batten on each end, so reduce the total length by 4″ and add the length of two ½″ tongues. This figure will be the lid length.

Square cut the 13-16″ thick lid to length, set up the dado with a ¼″ spacer raised to ½″ in height. Set the fence to center the tongue in the 13-16″ thickness. Mark an X on one surface, hold against the fence and pass over the dado, both ends of course. Cut away waste shoulder wood with a combination saw blade, leaving ½″ long tongues. Provide two batten pieces 13-16″ x 2″ x 2″ inches longer than the width of lid. Mount the two side dado cutters which make up ¼″ in width, raise to cut slightly better than ½″ in height, mark an X on one side of each batten. Set the fence to cut to the approximate center, nick a waste piece, check for matching placement with the tongues, make adjustment if necessary, hold X against fence and groove both pieces. Glue tongues and grooves, hand press in place, lay on two bar clamps and draw tight (photo 13-13). Remove the waste batten wood with the band saw. If there is extra wood in width, make a smoothing cut over the jointer on each long edge. Coarse sand both surfaces.

Before forming the lip, do the oval inlaying. Start with a longitudinal line down the center and a center cross line. Make a follow board for the large string oval by laying off on a ¼″ piece of plywood 1″ squares as indicated on the line drawing, having first marked the long and cross lines in pencil. Carefully pencil in the quarter oval over the squares, band or jig saw to this line, keeping the waste quarter intact for marking the remaining three sections. Saw the complete outline, place over crossed lines, use two clamps close to one end, bear against the router collar to cut the 1-16″ groove. Shift the clamps, one at a time, to the other half, finish groove cutting, glue inlay and seat (photo 13-14).

Prepare the center oval as explained in previous chapters, place on the crossed lines, scribe the outline, deepen with hand tools, rout close to the line, trim to the line with hand tools making a neat fit for the inlay (photo 13-15).

Gluing procedure follows previous chapters: glue recess, insert oval (paper side up), tape in place, cover with paper, place a ¾″ covering block and another hold-down piece clamped on each end (photo 13-14) and set overnight. Sand inlay to surface level.

Rabbet out the under side removing wood to leave 7-16″ deep and a lip ⅜″ wide. Make these cuts on the sides and top edges. Try for fit sideways; if there is not clearance of at least 1-16″ on each side, a rabbet plane will solve the problem. Hold the lid in place, check to see if the bottom corner meets the writing bed corner. Decide whether or not to take more wood from the bottom edge; there should be at least 1-16″ clearance at the top.

Clearance must be provided for the raised bead that borders the top drawer when the leaf is lowered. Before rounding the lip, make a ⅛″ x ⅛″ rabbet along the bottom upper corner (photo 13-4). Round the top corner all the way around the leaf and coarse sand the newly worked surfaces.

In conjunction with instructions for making the leaf, I believe it will be quite informative to study the photo of the open desk at the beginning of this chapter. Pencil mark the writing bed center in width and place a mark at 3″ and 4½″ from each end. Open the 1½″ hinges and lay one flat between the marks at one end, line the pin center along the writing bed edge, hold firmly in place and scribe its outline. Repeat at the other end and in the center. Set a ¼″ router bit to a depth twice the thickness of a hinge plate, route close to lines, finish waste removal with hand tools, fasten in place with just the one back ½″ screw of the proper number. Only one screw is used now because these hinges will have to be raised slightly at the pin to hold down level on the leaf for marking.

PHOTO 13–13

PHOTO 13–14

PHOTO 13–15

Photo 13 16

Photo 13-17

Photo 13-18

Extend the leaf supports, lay the leaf on supports and carefully center it from side to side. Press against the writing bed, hold down each hinge, scribe outline. Move the leaf away, rout, square out with hand tools, reposition and sink at least two of the three screws in each hinge half. Now be careful: slowly raise the leaf and keep watching the add-on radius blocks; if the lip ends appear to bind on the blocks, lower the leaf and shave off some of the block wood, and try again. Work with it until the lip follows nicely around the curve. When the leaf closes, there should be no scraping; if there is, try to work down the offending area with hand tools.

The best lock for the leaf is from Ball and Ball and is catalogued as style F 2¾″ wide x 2¼″ deep. These locks can also be used for the large drawers but smaller ones are preferable. Measure accurately for keyhole placement. Of course it must be centered from side to side and the critical point is down from the selvage. Cut the hole larger than the key, insert key from the outside, place lock pin in the key, and mark where to mortise for the lock. Both the back plate and the selvage must be mortised in flush with the surface wood. Inlay the ivory escutcheon. Make a strike plate for the lock bolt and mortise it in flush. Remove the leaf and finish sand all over.

Small drawer fronts are of ½″ thick wood cut to fit the openings. Sides, backs, and bottoms are of ¼″ thick poplar. The drawers extend back to within 5-16″ of the back pigeonhole line providing side surfaces to glue stop blocks. The fronts are inlaid with strings set in ⅛″ from edge. Chapter 14 explains drawer making in detail.

The large drawer fronts are 13-16″ thick and cut to fit the openings. ¼″ banding is inlaid all around the drawer fronts ¼″ in from the edges. Follow the mitering process that has been used in previous chapters. Photo 13-16 shows the corners squared out and inlay being seated. Photo 13-17 has the escutcheon inlaid and 13-18 shows a lock mortise made and ready to receive the lock. Sides, backs, and bottoms are ½″ poplar and extend back to within ½″ of the back rabbet allowing space for stop blocks which will be glued and nailed in place. Cut and fit the ¼″ plywood back.

Spend as much time as necessary going over the whole piece looking for areas missed when sanding or possible corners that should be smoothed better. I am sure you will be proud of this creation. Take your time finishing this piece and do a good job. Finishing techniques will be found in Chapter 15.

14

Dovetailing

DOVETAILING is the most satisfying and strongest method of making a joint where the grain of each piece runs to the corner of attachment.

Much of the confusion and uncertainty can be eliminated when one realizes that the same template is used for both the male and female parts. That means the shape, size, and even any unintentional curvature of an individual "tail" is unimportant because each piece is identically marked. When the "tail" is cut carefully to the scribed line and the corresponding cut-out to the matching line, any deviation from a straight line will be duplicated in each piece.

An abbreviated discourse on the choice of wood selected for drawer making will provide a better understanding of the series of photographs shown. The wood for drawer fronts is chosen first: look for color and grain pattern. Drawer fronts are nearly always a prominent part of a piece of furniture, so the material used for them is important. The next requirement, if the drawer is a deep or high one, is to look for warp across the grain. This will cause trouble and, at best, result in an unsatisfactory piece of work. Then, in the case of a long drawer (18″ and longer), check for longitudinal bow. It can readily be seen what this would do to a straight surrounding surface. The third and most important requisite is lack of twist. The longer the drawer, the more noticeable would be a slight twist. A good way to check for this unacceptable flaw is to hold the board up to eye level and place two straight edges, about 24″ in length, across the grain at each end; if they are parallel the piece is usable for a drawer front.

The interior poplar wood should also be selected with care. Warp and long bow are unacceptable conditions. When all materials are flawless, a perfect piece of work can be accomplished with ease.

DOVETAILING INFORMATION

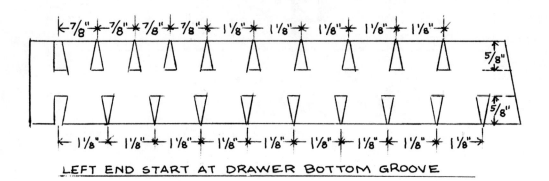

LEFT END START AT DRAWER BOTTOM GROOVE

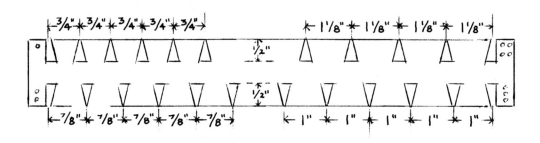

FOR VARYING HEIGHT DRAWER FRONTS

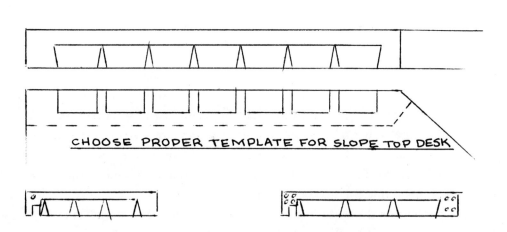

CHOOSE PROPER TEMPLATE FOR SLOPE TOP DESK

SMALL DRAWER FRONTS

Drawer wood thicknesses can be broken down to three divisions: large, deep drawers 27″ and more in length; fronts 13-16″; sides, backs, and bottoms ½″. Medium size, 15″ to 27″ in length; fronts ⅝″; sides, backs, and bottoms, ⅜″. Small pigeonhole size, fronts ½″; sides, backs, and bottoms ¼″ thick.

Before any dovetailing is done, all four pieces of a drawer (bottom not included) should be cut to size and, if the front happens to have a lip, that can be done so the shoulders will fit the opening. Determine and cut to the length and height of sides. Back length is to be exactly the length of front (if lipped) between shoulders; otherwise the same length as the front. In height, the back will be the same as the sides, less the thickness of the bottom board, plus ⅛″ clearance. An example: all drawers have ¼″ grooves in sides and fronts for the bottom tongue to slide in. The tongue is run on the top side of the bottom panel so for a planned ⅜″ bottom the groove must be ⅜″ plus ⅛″ above the bottom edge, which makes the back an even ½″ less in height than the sides.

Now let's talk about each photo and the drawing, where applicable. Photo 14-1 shows two aluminum strips of template that are duplicated on the line drawing to show sizes. The top edge of the top strip starts with ⅞″ between the first four tails and follows with the more or less standard 1⅛″ span. The reason for this difference can readily be seen when comparing the tails with the one on the lower edge. The template chosen would depend on the height of the drawer front. For example, it is possible that when holding the lower evenly divided one on a certain size front, it might leave nearly an inch of solid wood at the top edge. That would not be acceptable, so the template would be turned over and the other edge used. The left end of this strip is the starting end and the first tail cut-out is always held even with the top edge of groove.

The bottom strip is really four templates in one and one end of the four can be used for a drawer of any height with side wood ¼″ or ⅜″ thick. Set bevel gauge and scribe lines for cut-outs. Cut to these lines with tin snips. Remove the bottom line of V with a narrow cold chisel.

Photo 14-2 shows a scratch gauge set to the side wood thickness marking a drawer front end. All necessary markings for drawers with the same side wood thickness will have the same gauge setting. So the first marks are made on the front ends as shown. Those lines show where to hold the template for marking (photo 14-3). There is no need to mark the right angle because that line will be formed by the router depth.

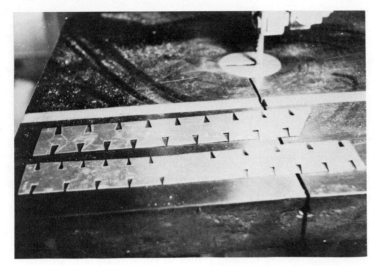

Photo 14-1

Photo 14-2

Photo 14-3

PHOTO 14-4

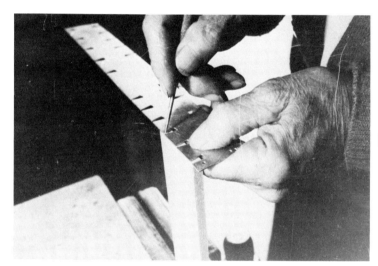

PHOTO 14-5

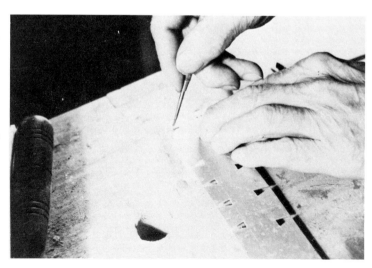

PHOTO 14-6

Next, both flat sides at both ends of each side and back piece must be gauge marked for template positioning (photo 14-4). When template marking, a starting point common to all parts must be selected. In the case of drawers, that point is the upper wall of groove for bottom board and is where the first tail will be placed when marking the fronts and sides. The back piece starts just above the groove so the template is placed at the back bottom edge (photo 14-5). Template markings have been made on the front and back piece ends but the sides must be laid flat with the groove side up and template placed just above the groove (photo 14-6).

Years ago I hesitated recommending the use of a portable router because, at that time, very few were included in home workshop equipment and even fewer owners had enough experience in their use. In previous books, I suggested chopping out the wood between tails on drawer fronts, a method that was safer but much more time-consuming.

Observe carefully photos 14-7 and 14-8. Routing out for the tails requires an adequate area so the router base will not rock. What is shown is a supplemental board clamped to the drawer front, increasing the area and extending past each end. The front shown in photo 14-7 is one of the larger lipped drawers for Chapter 10. Both photos show the fence set to rout to the gauge line and side piece thickness in depth. WARNING! Routing into end wood requires unusually firm control of router movement. Hand tool carefully to the scribed lines (photo 14-9).

After the fronts are cut, the backs are tail marked on the ends and scratch gauged on each side for length of tails (photo 14-10). Pencil mark the place to saw on each side of the tails for waste wood removal. Photo 14-11 shows a back piece sawn to the pencil lines. The middle one has the first waste cut made and the last piece has all the waste removed by the jig saw where they are lying.

Photos 14-12 and 14-13 show side pieces on the jig saw table sawn for tail cut-outs. This step is followed by completing the cut-outs with a narrow chisel and mallet (photos 14-14 and 14-15). Finish hand tooling back piece ends as shown on photo 14-16.

If the fronts have lips, either quarter round or thumbnail the outside corner edges before sanding all drawer parts. Sand coarse and fine front face surfaces, both sides of side pieces, and the inside of backs. Before gluing the drawers

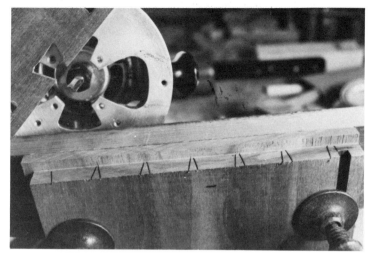

Photo 14–7

Photo 14–8

Photo 14–9

Photo 14–10

Photo 14–11

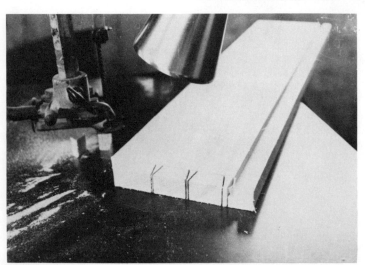

Photo 14–12

Photo 14-13

Photo 14-14

Photo 14-15

Photo 14–16

Photo 14–17

Photo 14–18

Photo 14-19

Photo 14-20

Photo 14-21

together, check for side piece heights; if they bind, either saw or joint to fit. Glue only the tails when assembling the drawers, line up each joint by hand, and use a waste block and large hammer to seat the side piece tightly. Insert in opening and, if it should be too tight to go all the way in, try to find where wood must be removed. A slight bind is acceptable until the glue is set overnight. The drawer must be inserted full depth to be sure it is square with the opening.

Drawer bottom panels can be glued to width with the grain running the long way. Finish sizing, rough sand top surface, run ¼″ tongues, slide in place, and sink three holding nails through the bottom into the back piece. Now finish fitting the drawer by sliding it in and out to check for tight spots; if any exist, try to find and remove with hand tools. If drawers have lips, no stop blocks are necessary; if not, a block glued and nailed at each end is required. Photos 14-17 through 14-21 show additional views or angles to help you in the dovetailing procedure.

Do not cut dovetails to go through wood thicker than ½″. It is possible to do so but the necessity for increasingly accurate fitting is out of all proportion to the extra thickness. When two pieces of 13-16″ thick wood are to be joined by dovetailing, proceed as was suggested for the Slope-Top Desk top board. That was done by cutting away shoulder wood to leave ½″ x ½″ wood for the tail cut-outs.

One final comment on butt glue joints. Sometime you may read that the best way to make a butt joint is to bore for dowels every so many inches. The only advantage of this is to keep the two pieces from falling apart if and when the joint should separate. Also a tongue and groove joint is no stronger than a plain butt joint when the grain in both pieces runs parallel.

15

Finishing and Allied Operations

SANDING

THOROUGH SANDING is one of the most important operations when making good furniture and the quality of the sandpaper used is equally important. The use of "Flint" papers will dishearten every hobbyist who tries them. Find a supplier in your locality who stocks "Garnet" cabinet finishing papers.

The term "coarse or rough sand" used frequently here pertains to the sandpaper grit which is #60 and the normal procedure for this coarse work. "Fine or finish sand" employs #120 grit and usually follows the coarse sanding with #60.

Garnet papers are standard 9″ x 11″ size sheets. To reduce a sheet to working size, fold, crease, and tear in half. Fold, crease, and tear one of these halves again, to get two pieces each 4½″ x 5½″. For block sanding, provide a block of sheet cork (1st choice), or semi hard rubber, or a soft wood sized to about 3″ x 4″ x ¾″. Cover the bottom of the block with paper, folding it up the sides and grip for comfortable sanding action.

For flat work, such as table tops, use #60 grit on a block and start with a natural stroke that may be ten, twelve, or even more inches long. Choose the near corner to commence this invigorating exercise, gradually work your way across the width and, just as slowly, work your way back. Move half a length forward and repeat, continuing the routine for the entire surface. This may or may not be sufficient for the coarse paper. Until you are much more familiar with sanding in general, try a piece of the primary wood about 12″ square, sand this exactly as you would your furniture piece each step of the way and, when you believe it to be ready for finishing materials, put the trial piece through the process to learn how well you did your homework.

When making any piece of furniture, it is well to look ahead as construction proceeds to the sanding that must be done. You should decide whether or not to sand each part, as it is worked on, and how much, before assembly. Usually it is much easier to sand in the open, if possible, rather than after pockets or inside corners have been formed.

As part of your equipment, sanding sticks are well worth the time it takes to make them. Three basic shapes will serve for general purpose work. Make one about 7″ long x ½″ wide x 3-16″ thick. Leave a ½″ side flat and crown the other to leave about 1-16″ edges. Another stick, 7″ long x ¾″ wide x ¼″ thick, is made into a wedge shape, ¼″ thick at one edge, tapered to 1-16″ at the other edge. Also have a few lengths of dowel rod of appropriate diameter to meet the needs of the moment. To use a stick, wrap one half of a quarter sheet of sandpaper tightly around the stick and hold it tight when you use it.

FINISHING MATERIALS

The finishing process starts with a wood stain so we will talk about stain as it pertains to the inlaid furniture discussed in this book. Not long ago we called it oil stain; now, with petroleum in short supply, manufacturers are calling the substitute "wood stain." Like any substitute material, the stain does not come up to the original, but one must learn how to use it to the best advantage. No specific brands are mentioned because, by the time this book is printed and released, the manufacturers may have changed the formulas. Three basic colors are needed: medium dark brown that may be called a nice walnut; a tan color that probably would be called light oak; and a red mahogany that, before blending, is in most cases an atrocious color.

With furniture other than inlaid, colors may be blended any way that seems desirable, but when the piece is inlaid, stain shades must be kept on the light side so the inlay woods will not be colored too much. That is why most of the subject pieces here are made of walnut to furnish natural color contrast although the Sewing Table and Lady's Desk are of cherry. The Pembroke Table and Martha Washington Chair are of mahogany.

The same pleasing mix of colors can be used for both walnut and cherry. The probable proportions for most brands would be: ⅓ each of brown, tan and slowly add red for desired color and shade.

If you are working with inlaid mahogany, a different coloring material must be used because the popular color and shade of the primary wood is a medium reddish brown and the wood stain used for other woods would darken the inlays too much. Sodium bichromate (orange colored crystals) dissolved in water and used as a water stain will result in a pleasing color. If you are unfamiliar with this material, do some experimenting. A weak solution will probably be what you will settle for. The final resulting color will not be seen until the solution is brushed on, dried thoroughly, and coated with a sanding sealer. It is interesting to watch how the solution gradually changes from a weak orange tinge to a dull uninteresting brown until it is coated with sealer.

Sodium bichromate can be used on other woods also but with disappointing results. It will deepen the natural color of the wood but not uniformly. If two or more pieces of cherry are glued together, one piece may dry darker than the other. It is used primarily because most of the woods comprising inlay designs are only slightly affected by the solution.

Common water stains are not mentioned here because the results are about the same as with "wood stain" and they do raise the grain much more, requiring more time and effort sanding for subsequent material coats.

Sanding sealer or shellac cut in half with solvent follows the stain. Lacquer, varnish or varnish substitutes will complete material applications.

The normal procedural sequence is as follows: apply stain with a brush. Delayed wiping with a cloth will deepen the stain shade. Best results will be obtained if wiped stain is allowed to dry overnight.

Spray or brush on sanding sealer next. Spray equipment is used much more now than it was years ago and, of course, does a better job than a brush. Waiting overnight or until thoroughly dry is a must for the sealer coat because a critical sanding with 7/0 finishing garnet paper takes place at this time, leaving the surfaces satin-smooth. A white powdery residue should be left on the surfaces after sanding if the sealer was dry enough to sand.

For mahogany only, a dark brown paste filler is the next step. Reduce filler with mineral spirits to brushing consistency, use a soft cloth in a circular motion, ending with straight strokes with the grain, to be followed, when dry, with another sealer coat, 7/0 sanding.

Almost everyone prefers a specific final coating material. The only requirement is that it be colorless. If it is fast drying like lacquer, a spray gun is indicated. Slower drying materials may be either brushed or sprayed and, in my opinion, the concentration of all final materials should be reduced about half with solvent. This reduction necessitates more coatings for the same amount of solids build-up but the result is worth the extra effort. Well-worn 7/0 paper sanding between thoroughly dried coats should leave you with a most satisfying feeling of a job well done.

Rub the last coat lightly when dry with #000 steel wool and, finally, apply a furniture polish of your choice but be sure to wipe all surfaces dry.

There is no particular problem with mounting brass hardware. If two of the larger drawer pulls are necessary, there is no formula for how far from the ends to place them. Lay the plates on a front, shift them to a position you like and mark for post holes.

The best brass hardware (Ball and Ball) is worth the added cost and will enhance the appearance of your work immensely.